WILL WE HAVE JEWISH GRANDCHILDREN?
Jewish Continuity and How to Achieve it

JONATHAN SACKS

VALLENTINE MITCHELL

First published in 1994 in Great Britain by
VALLENTINE MITCHELL & CO. LTD
Newbury House, 900 Eastern Avenue, Newbury Park
Ilford, Essex IG2 7HH, England

Copyright © 1994 Jonathan Sacks

British Library Cataloguing in Publication Data

Sacks, Jonathan
 Will We Have Jewish Grandchildren?
 Jewish Continuity and How to Achieve it
 I. Title
 305.8924

ISBN 0-85303-282-3

Library of Congress Cataloging-in-Publication Data

Sacks, Jonathan, Rabbi.
  Will we have Jewish grandchildren? : Jewish continuity and how to achieve it / Jonathan Sacks.
    p. cm.
  Includes bibliographical references and index.
  ISBN 0-85303-282-3
  1. Judaism—Great Britain. 2. Jews—Great Britain—Cultural assimilation. 3. Judaism–20th century. I. Title.
BM292.S23 1994
296'.094'09049—dc20   94-10416
                                                        CIP

ISBN 0-85303-282-3

All rights reserved. No part of this publication may be reproduced in any form or by any means, electronic, mechanical, photocopying, recording or otherwise, without the prior permission of Vallentine Mitchell & Co. Ltd.

Typeset by Vitaset, Paddock Wood
Printed in Great Britain by
Redwood Books, Trowbridge, Wiltshire

WILL WE HAVE JEWISH GRANDCHILDREN?

By the same author

TORAH STUDIES

TRADITION AND TRANSITION
(*editor*)

TRADITION IN AN UNTRADITIONAL AGE

ARGUMENTS FOR THE SAKE OF HEAVEN

ORTHODOXY CONFRONTS MODERNITY
(*editor*)

THE PERSISTENCE OF FAITH:
Religion, Morality and Society in a Secular Age

CRISIS AND COVENANT:
Jewish thought after the Holocaust

ONE PEOPLE?
Tradition, Modernity and Jewish Unity

*For Joshua, Dina and Gila –
our Jewish continuity*

Contents

Acknowledgements

Introduction 1
1 The Miracle 6
2 The Crisis 17
3 The Secret 31
4 Testing the Hypothesis 41
5 Priorities 49
6 From Integration to Survival to Continuity 63
7 Segregation? 75
8 Israel and the Diaspora 86
9 From Jewish Continuity to *Jewish Continuity* 101
10 Epilogue 112
Appendix: The Structure of Continuity 117
Bibliography 124
Index 129

Acknowledgements

This book has emerged, not from a merely theoretical inquiry but from an urgent practical concern: how to create a new organisation with the potential to transform a diaspora community, Anglo-Jewry, and set it on the road to renewal.

It is rare for a practical initiative to be launched by a book. In this case, however, in order for *Jewish Continuity* to succeed as an organisation we need to understand Jewish continuity as a concept, and the historical background which has made it suddenly problematic. In my thinking I have been helped by many individuals who have reflected on Anglo-Jewry and its needs, and I wish here to record my thanks.

My predecessor as Chief Rabbi, Lord Jakobovits, did much to prepare the groundwork. He established the Jewish Educational Development Trust in 1971 and his campaign, 'Let My People Know', placed education firmly on the Anglo-Jewish agenda.

My realisation that a new structure was needed for the 1990s originated in a conversation, three years ago, with Rabbi Shlomo Levin and Michael Cohen, two individuals who have done more than most to develop outreach and education in Anglo-Jewry.

Stanley and Carole Simmonds lent my family their lovely home in Jerusalem for the months preceding my taking up office, and it was there, overlooking the Old City, that the miracle of Jewish continuity and renewal captured my imagination. During my stay in Israel I had many conversations with Simon Caplan which began the process of evolving a practical strategy. Professor Seymour Fox, Alan Hoffman and Annette Hochstein of the Mandel Institute in Jerusalem lent their immense expertise in educational planning, and helped us to formulate the right questions.

All thinking on the future of Anglo-Jewry owes a special debt to Stanley Kalms and Fred Worms. The Kalms Report on the United Synagogue, *A Time for Change* (1992), and the Jewish Education Development Trust (J.E.D.T.) Report chaired by Fred Worms, *Securing our Future* (1992), provided detailed research on the current state of synagogue life and Jewish education, as well as imaginative prescriptions for change. Together, these two reports created the climate for a

Will we have Jewish Grandchildren?

Continuity initiative, and our plans are set out against the backdrop of their conclusions.

The creation of a new organisation raises the spectre of battles for turf and territory. We were therefore fortunate to have, throughout, the support of the leaders of Anglo-Jewry's other major communal bodies. Sir Trevor Chinn and Cyril Stein of the Joint Israel Appeal, and Lord Young of Graffham and Michael Levy of Jewish Care, helped us think through the problems of launching a new communal structure and gave freely of their advice. Michael Phillips, chairman of the Jewish Educational Development Trust, was unfailingly generous in his encouragement, as were Seymour Saideman, President of the United Synagogue, and Judge Israel Finestein, President of the Board of Deputies. Alan Fox, Melvyn Carlowe and Morton Creeger gave valuable professional counsel.

We could not have set up *Jewish Continuity* without the efforts of Michael Mail and Syma Weinberg of the J.E.D.T., who did much of the early professional work, as did Lira Winston of the Sinclair Montrose Trust and Rhoda Goodman of my office. Their dedication was exceptional.

No less remarkable was the help provided by a formidably gifted group of lay-people, each of whom contributed to the thinking and momentum of the initiative. Among them were Richard Alberg, Michael Bradfield, Charles Corman, Tony Danker, Norman Finegold, Allan Fisher, Sidney Frosh, Professor Martin Gilbert, Michael Goldmeier, Barbara Green, Stephen Greenman, Henry Israel, Brian Kerner, Henry Knobil, Alan Lee, Lynndy Levin, Daniel Levy, Peter Levy, Richard Loftus, Andrew Loftus, John Martin, Benjamin Perl, Rosalind Preston, Joshua Rowe, Professor David Hillel Ruben, Rob Sumroy and Professor Leslie Wagner.

We could not have proceeded without the support of leading figures in the Anglo-Jewish community. Special thanks are due to Stanley Cohen, Sidney Corob, Dr David Khalili, Clive Marks, Dame Shirley Porter, Felix Posen, Sir Harry Solomon, Lord Woolf, Lord (David) Wolfson and Lord (Leonard) Wolfson, whose encouragement strengthened our conviction that *Jewish Continuity* was the necessary project for our time.

To these must be added the many educators, rabbis, youth leaders and outreach workers from all sections of the Anglo-Jewish community with whom we consulted before setting up the organisation, and whose views further clarified our plans.

Acknowledgements

I am grateful to Frank Cass of Vallentine Mitchell for agreeing to publish this work, along with other studies in Jewish renewal, and to Teddy Reitman for assisting the publications of our office. The manuscript was read by, among others, Dayan Ivan Binstock, Charles Corman, Judge Israel Finestein, John Martin and Professor Leslie Wagner, all of whom offered valuable suggestions and criticisms.

Two individuals, though, stand out for the sheer weight of their contribution. The first is Jonathan Kestenbaum, Executive Director of the Office of the Chief Rabbi. *Jewish Continuity* is as much his creation as mine. Since we first met, six months before we took up our respective positions, we have been engaged in continuous dialogue about the theory and practice of Jewish renewal. Intuitively, in those early days, I sensed that we would need to create something like *Continuity*, and that Jonathan was the person to do it. He has exceeded even those high hopes, and brought the project to fruition with commitment and panache.

The second is Dr Michael Sinclair, *Jewish Continuity*'s first chairman. Michael, a psychiatrist turned successful businessman, sat with astonishing calm throughout our first meeting as I asked him to create, from nothing, the biggest project in recent Anglo-Jewish history. After I had finished my lengthy exposition, he gave me his reply. It consisted of one word: Yes. I was not sure then whether he knew what he was letting himself in for, and perhaps neither was he. Ever since, he has not only allocated vast amounts of time to the project but, more importantly, he has lent it the colouring of his unique personality, inventive, receptive and creative, practical and intellectual at once, and driven throughout by a deep thirst for spirituality and personal Jewish growth.

Finally, I must acknowledge the role played by Clive Lawton, appointed as I was preparing this final draft to be *Continuity*'s first Chief Executive. His colourful, unconventional approach to Jewish education augurs well for the future of the organisation as a source of innovation in Anglo-Jewry and as one that genuinely reaches out to Jews wherever they are.

May *Continuity*'s success be their reward, and the renewal of Anglo-Jewry ours.

Introduction

This book, the first I have written since becoming Chief Rabbi, is written with a sense of grave urgency.

In my most recently published book, *One People?*, I spoke about the three conflicts that currently divide the Jewish people, threatening to split it apart. One is the war of cultures between religious and secular Jews, which rages in Israel and flares up sporadically in Jewries elsewhere. Another is the slow separation of Israel and the diaspora, something we will notice increasingly in the coming years. The third, and the one which dominated the book, was the intractable schism between Orthodoxy and liberal interpretations of Judaism.

These were the conflicts which dominated the Jewish landscape when I wrote the book at the end of 1988. They were still there when I redrafted it shortly before my installation in 1991. They remain, and have not diminished since. But there is an ancient parable of the rabbis about Jewish history:

> To what is it like? It is like a man who was travelling on the road when he encountered a wolf and escaped from it, and he went along relating the affair of the wolf. He then encountered a lion and escaped from it, and went along relating the affair of the lion. He then encountered a snake and escaped from it, whereupon he forgot the two previous incidents and went along relating the affair of the snake. So it is with Israel. The latter troubles make them forget the earlier ones.

A fourth problem has arisen which threatens to overwhelm all else and make other conflicts marginal by comparison. The great divide in the future will not be between secular and religious Jews, or between Israel and the diaspora, or between Orthodoxy and Reform. It will be between those who will remain Jews and those who will not.

Shimon Peres, Israel's Foreign Minister, put it simply on a recent visit to London. A few years ago, he said, Jews throughout the world were split over the question of 'Who is a Jew?' Is a Jew one who has a Jewish mother, as *halakhah* insists? Or is a Jew also one who has a Jewish father, as American Reform maintains? In the future, he said, we will have to adopt a third definition. A Jew will not be one who has a Jewish mother or father. *A Jew will be one who has Jewish children.*

He was referring to the dramatic rise of intermarriage in the diaspora. Within a generation, mixed marriage has escalated with a speed that has taken observers by surprise and it now threatens the very basis of Jewish survival in one community after another throughout the world. The Jewish family – two Jews who decide to marry, have Jewish children, and thus continue the Jewish heritage – has suddenly become fragile. As a result, the great chain of Jewish tradition, stretching across three-quarters of the history of human civilisation, is in danger of breaking. The future of diaspora Jewry is at risk.

This is not an over-statement. Anglo-Jewry, estimated at 450,000 Jews in the 1950s, now numbers barely 300,000. That means we have lost more than ten Jews a day, every day, for the last forty years. The significance of this is more than demographic. Certainly, it means that our community is shrinking, ageing and declining, but it means more than that. It means that young Jews are disengaging, disaffiliating and drifting away from Judaism. This is something that touches our very soul. Paul Johnson begins his monumental *A History of the Jews* with the sentence, 'The Jews are the most tenacious people in history.' That is true no longer. We are losing the collective will to live as Jews.

Fortunately, however, the Jewish people has never been led by behavioural scientists. We are a kingdom of priests, not an assembly of sociologists. We have never taken trends as inevitable, nor have we mistaken facts for commandments. We can, I believe, reverse the decline, but on two conditions. The first is that we understand our present situation. We must look at what is happening to young Jews and ask why. The second is that we summon the collective will to make good the shortcomings of contemporary Jewish life. They are many and deep.

Fortunately too, though we are a fractious people, crisis unites us. As the rabbis said: when it comes to the history of Jewish suffering, 'The latter troubles make us forget the earlier ones'. The entire book of Genesis is taken up with arguments within the family, between husbands and wives, parents and children, and between siblings. But as soon as the book of Exodus begins, the Israelites are faced with exile and slavery, and for the first time we hear the phrase *am bnei Yisrael*, 'the people of the children of Israel'. Earlier rivalries have been forgotten, and a divided family has become a united people.

We face crisis, a crisis of continuity. It can be defined by a simple question and a far from simple answer. The question is: *Will we have*

Jewish grandchildren? The answer is: Yes – *if*. This book, and others I hope to write on the subject, are about the *if* of continuity.

It is not a single *if* because Jewish life has many dimensions. There is the community and its institutions and priorities. There is the Jewish home and the atmosphere of family life we construct. And there are the individuals who make up our families and communities. How they understand and live their Jewishness will have a bearing on how the next generation chooses to live theirs. Each of these dimensions is a crucial component of Jewish continuity and will affect whether it succeeds or fails. But they are different from one another and cannot be dealt with in the same language or frame of reference.

This book is about only one of these dimensions, the Jewish community. It asks what we must do *as a collective body* – as Anglo-Jewry – to ensure that our children will choose to live, marry and have children as Jews. It is less about identity and faith – things that concern us as families and individuals – than about communal strategy and priorities. I hope to write about these other perspectives, but not here.

My argument is simple. We are entering a new era in modern Jewish history. The past two hundred years have been dominated, for Jews, by two concerns: *integration* into the societies of Europe and America, and *survival* against the onslaughts of antisemitism and the Holocaust. The 1990s will be seen in retrospect as the beginning of a new phase, one in which the predominant concern became the *continuity* of Jewish identity against the background of assimilation and intermarriage in the diaspora and secularisation in the State of Israel.

My belief is that just as Jews collectively succeeded in integrating and surviving, so we will succeed in renewing the bases of our continuity. But just as the first two challenges involved a profound struggle within the Jewish soul, so will the third. *Am Yisrael*, the Jewish people, derives its name from the moment when Jacob wrestled with an angel and was told that his name would henceforth be Israel, 'for you have wrestled with God and with man and have prevailed'. Israel would be the people that had to engage in inner conflict before it could prevail. It still is.

The particular challenge facing us – in Anglo-Jewry, in the diaspora generally, and even in the State of Israel – is to determine whether or not Jewish identity can be sustained in an open, secular society. It can – but not without a determined effort to rebuild the vehicles, the transmitters, of Jewish continuity. For the past two hundred years, these have been neglected, because the battlefront was elsewhere. The greatest single danger is not that we do not know *how* to create continuity, but that we will fail to do so because we did not recognise that times have changed, and so too has the challenge. By continuing to fight yesterday's battles, we risk losing the battle of today. There must be a massive shift in our communal priorities and strategy. For this to happen, we must understand what is at stake, and what have been the transformations of Jewish life in our time. That is what this book seeks to explain. We must also understand what is old and what is new in the concept of continuity. In one sense, continuity is Judaism's oldest challenge. Handing on a tradition, a way of life and an identity is what successive generations have done since the days of Abraham and Sarah, with a persistence that has no rival in the chronicles of human civilisation. But how to do so in an age in which Jewish identity has become weak, fragmented and confused is altogether more difficult. It is a predicament which we have faced only rarely in our past. It is this that marks our time as a new era in Jewish history.

The task before us is part intellectual, part practical. We must understand. But we must also act. The rabbis of old were devoted to study. They spent their days arguing and analysing our sacred texts, and most of their nights as well. But they also said: 'Great is learning for it leads to doing.' Study is not an academic enterprise only. It is the preface to action, and therein lies its power.

If this is true of individuals, it is true of a community as well. Accordingly, though much in this book is taken up with reflection, it ends with a summons to collective action. It accompanies the launch of a new Anglo-Jewish organisation, *Jewish Continuity*, whose task will be to take the vision set forth in these pages and turn it into reality. This study is therefore more than a theoretical analysis. It is a prelude to a long and practical engagement with the greatest Jewish challenge of our time.

That challenge is defined by Alan Dershowitz at the end of his book *Chutzpah*:

> We have survived – sometimes by the skin of our teeth – millennia of rape attempts against the Jewish body and soul by villains and monsters of every description. Efforts to convert us, assimilate us, and exterminate us by the sword have taken an enormous toll, but in the end they have failed. Now the dangers are more subtle: willing seduction, voluntary assimilation, deliberate abdication. We have learned – painfully and with difficulty – how to fight others. Can we develop Jewish techniques for defending against our own success?

That is the question. *Jewish Continuity* is our answer. Between the two, though, lies a journey, one that will force us to think about the very nature of Jewish existence now and against the backdrop of eternity. It begins with a mystery, perhaps even a miracle. What *is* Jewish continuity?

1
The Miracle

In the Cairo Museum stands a giant slab of black granite known as the Merneptah stele. Originally installed by Pharaoh Amenhotep III in his temple in western Thebes, it was removed by a later ruler of Egypt, Merneptah, who reigned in the thirteenth century BCE. Inscribed with hieroglyphics, it contains a record of Merneptah's military victories. Its interest might have been confined to students of ancient civilisations, were it not for one fact: the stele contains the first reference outside the Bible to the people of Israel. What does it tell us about our ancestors and how they appeared to others? The inscription lists the various powers crushed by Merneptah and his army. It concludes:

> All lands together, they are pacified;
> Everyone who was restless, he has been bound
> By the King of Upper and Lower Egypt . . .

Among those who were 'restless' were a small people otherwise unmentioned in the early Egyptian texts. Merneptah or his chroniclers believed that they were now a mere footnote to history. They had not simply been defeated. They had been obliterated. This is what the stele says:

> Israel is laid waste, his seed is not.

The first reference to Israel outside the Bible is an obituary notice. Ironically, so is the second. This is contained in a basalt slab dating from the ninth century BCE which today stands in the Louvre. Known as the Mesha stele, it records the triumphs of Mesha, king of Moab. The king thanks his deity Chemosh for handing victory to the Moabites in their wars, and speaks thus: 'As for Omri, king of Israel, he humbled Moab many years, for Chemosh was angry with his land. And his son followed him and he also said, "I will humble Moab." In my time he spoke thus, but I have triumphed over him and over his house, while *Israel has perished forever.*'

The story of Jewish survival is so strange, unique and vast that it strains our imagination to the limit. Even the events of a single century, our own, defy sober description. The twentieth century of the Common Era – the fifty-seventh century, Jewish time – witnessed the most brutal, systematic assault on the Jewish people since ancient times: the Third Reich's Final Solution in which the whole of European Jewry was scheduled for destruction and in which six million Jews, one third of world Jewry, perished. Yet, the Jewish response to the Holocaust has been the rebirth of the State of Israel, the restoration of Jewish sovereignty after a lapse of nineteen hundred years and the ingathering of Jews from more than seventy countries to their ancestral home.

More than 3,000 years ago Moses, at the end of his life, addressed the assembled Israelites in the desert. They had not yet crossed the Jordan. Their history as a people in their own land had not yet begun. In world terms, they were an insignificant group of erstwhile slaves, a potential irritant to other powers but no more. None the less, as he reviewed the events that they had lived through, Moses was convinced that this people and its story would endure to the end of time. He foresaw no comfortable destiny for his people. When he turned to the future, he did not speak of a mighty civilisation, economically strong and militarily invincible. Moses' speech is entirely free of the triumphalism that marks the records of other leaders of the ancient world. Israel, he predicted, would remain a tiny people. It would frequently be at the mercy of greater powers. It would be led astray by affluence. Its people would lose the one thing that made them different, even remarkable: their faith in and dedication to God. They would suffer defeats and exile and persecution. But they would remain distinctive. They would endure. And one day, 'Even if you have been banished to the most distant land under the heavens', God would bring them back.

At the very beginnings of their national history Moses recognised that there would never be any other people quite like Israel. Turning to the new generation, he asked them a rhetorical question:

For ask now of the days past, which were before thee, since the day that God created man upon the earth, and from one end of heaven unto the other, whether there hath been any such thing as this great thing is, or hath been heard like it?

That question still echoes, gathering force with each successive century.

Today, as the twentieth century draws to its close and as we stand as if on a mountain peak surveying the breathtaking landscape of Jewish history, we know this: that those who sought to destroy the people of the covenant gather dust in the museums of mankind while *am Yisrael chai*, the people Israel lives. Ancient Egypt is no more. The Moabites have long since disappeared. The Assyrians, Babylonians, Persians, Greeks and Romans successively strode the stage of world dominion. Each empire played its part, said its lines, and each in turn has gone. In our day, the two great powers which declared 'Israel is laid waste, his seed is not' – the Third Reich and the Soviet Union – have been defeated, dismantled and have disappeared. But the Jews survive. 'Ask now of the days past, which were before thee, since the day that God created man upon the earth . . . whether there hath been any such thing as this great thing is, or hath been heard like it?'

WITNESSES

Perhaps we are too close to appreciate to the full the majestic, improbable persistence of the Jewish people. We speak, after all, of *our* people, our grandparents and theirs back across the generations. Wonders are more awesome when we come upon them from afar, but this wonder is no further away than our own family tree were we able to trace it back four thousand years through space and time.

Perhaps, too, we are victims of our own astonishing faith. For never once, even in our remotest past, did we doubt that Israel would be a people of eternity. In a passage of almost unrelieved darkness, Moses foresees the devastation that would befall Israel if it departed from its sacred vocation. But at the end of this prophecy of suffering, he adds in the name of God. 'Yet in spite of this, when they are in the land of their enemies, I will not reject them or abhor them so as to destroy them completely, breaking My covenant with them.' Isaiah declares that though Israel will be deeply afflicted, 'a remnant will return'. Jeremiah, in cascading poetry, solemnly affirms the immortality of Israel:

> This is what the Lord says,
> He who appoints the sun to shine by day,
> Who decrees the moon and stars
> To shine by night,
> Who stirs up the sea
> So that its waves roar –
> The Lord Almighty is His name:

> 'Only if these decrees vanish from My sight,'
> declares the Lord,
> 'Will the descendants of Israel ever cease
> To be a nation before me.'

Jews never doubted the truth of the momentous blessing we make over the Torah, in which we thank God 'who gave us the Torah of truth and thus planted within us eternal life'. No one has put this sense of certainty better than Paul Johnson at the culmination of his *A History of the Jews*:

> If the earliest Jews were able to survey, with us, the history of their progeny, they would find nothing surprising in it. They always knew that Jewish society was appointed to be a pilot-project for the entire human race. That Jewish dilemmas, dramas and catastrophes should be exemplary, larger than life, would seem only natural to them. That Jews should over the millennia attract such unparalleled, indeed inexplicable, hatred would be regrettable but only to be expected. Above all, that the Jews should still survive, when all those other ancient people were transmuted or vanished into the oubliettes of history, was wholly predictable. How could it be otherwise? Providence decreed it and the Jews obeyed.

The most eloquent witnesses to the miracle of Israel are therefore not Jews but those who came upon our history from the outside. Blaise Pascal was one. In his *Pensées*, he wrote:

> Whereas the peoples of Greece and Italy . . . have long since perished, these [the Jews] still survive, and, despite the endeavours of so many mighty kings who have over and over again sought to destroy them, as their historians testify and as it is easy to deduce by the natural course of things, they have nevertheless been preserved all through these many years (and their preservation was a thing foretold), and, stretching from their earliest to the latest times, their history embraces all others.

The Russian thinker Nicolas Berdyayev was another who was transfixed by his study of Jewish history. In *The Meaning of History* he confesses that it forced him to jettison his preconceptions of the laws governing the fate of nations. As a Marxist, he had believed that the destiny of civilisations was ruled by material forces: economies, wars, the physical indices of power. But in the case of Jewry he found a people whose fate could only be accounted for in non-material terms. As the prophet Zechariah had said, and as he now discovered, here was a people who endured 'Not by might nor by power but by My spirit'.

Berdyayev was led to the following admission:

I remember how the materialist interpretation of history, when I attempted in my youth to verify it by applying it to the destinies of peoples, broke down in the case of the Jews, where destiny seemed absolutely inexplicable from the materialistic standpoint ... Its survival is a mysterious and wonderful phenomenon demonstrating that the life of this people is governed by a special predetermination, transcending the processes of adaptation expounded by the materialistic interpretation of history. The survival of the Jews, their resistance to destruction, their endurance under absolutely peculiar conditions and the fateful role played by them in history: all these point to the particular and mysterious foundations of their destiny.

Friedrich Nietzsche, the most radical thinker of the nineteenth century, and Karl Barth, modern Christianity's leading neo-traditionalist theologian, had no such sympathy for the Jews. Nietzsche was a hostile and relentless critic of Judaism. Necessarily so, for he saw in Judaism the origin of the ethical imperative in Western civilisation, which he sought to overthrow in the name of the will to power. None the less he candidly admitted that 'The Jews are the most remarkable nation of world history' because, 'faced with the question of being or not being', they always chose to live as Jews even without power rather than ally themselves with power at the cost of ceasing to be Jews.

In the shadow of the Holocaust, Karl Barth wrote about Jewish suffering. His *Church Dogmatics* is painful to read, for in it he reaffirms one of the most ominous of traditional Christian doctrines, that the trials and tribulations of Jews are the price they pay for refusing to become Christians. 'This,' he writes, 'is how Israel punishes itself for its sectarian self-assertion.' None the less even he is moved to admit that 'The existence of the Jews, as is generally recognised, is an adequate proof of the existence of God.' Consciously or unwittingly he was echoing a famous precedent. It is said that King Frederic the Great once asked a Lutheran clergyman to provide him with a proof of God's existence. The pastor replied: 'Your majesty, the Jews.'

A SINGULAR PEOPLE

It was not simply that Jews survived. So too did the Chinese. So, as Arnold Toynbee pointed out, did the Parsees. It was that Jews survived without any of the normal accompaniments of survival. For most of their history, they had neither land nor power. They were driven into exile. They were dispersed across the face of the globe. Time after time they were uprooted. In the Middle Ages, Jews were expelled from

England in 1290, from France in 1306 and 1394, from Vienna and Linz in 1421, from Cologne in 1424, from Perugia in 1485, from Milan in 1489, from Florence and Tuscany in 1494, and most dramatically and traumatically from Spain in 1492.

They had no common territory. Other than Hebrew, the language of prayer, they had no common language. Nor did they share a culture. Rashi lived in Christian France. Maimonides was born in Islamic Spain. One spoke French, the other Arabic. Their worlds were utterly different. Rashi inhabited the atmosphere of anti-Jewish hostility that was soon to explode in the massacres of the Crusades. Maimonides lived in the high intellectual altitude of Islamic neo-Aristotelianism. They were as far apart as were Western and Eastern European Jewry in the nineteenth century. All that linked them was a faith, a way of life, a memory and a hope. No people has ever been held together by such slender threads. Yet they proved stronger than steel.

Nor, contrary to the history of other great civilisations, did the Jews flourish once and then decline. Time and again they faced crisis and responded with stunning bursts of creativity. Always at or near the centre of world events, they faced opposition and hostility, first from the great empires of the ancient world – Egypt, Assyria, Babylon and Persia – then from the Greeks and Romans, then during the Middle Ages from Christianity and Islam, and most recently from the two great secular totalitarianisms, Fascism and Communism. At each phase they discovered new modes of spirituality from within themselves. Prophets and priests were succeeded by scribes and then sages, and in turn by commentators, jurists, poets, philosophers, mystics and pioneers of the return to Zion.

When the gates of wider culture and society were opened to them, within a generation the Jews had produced from their ranks scientists, statesmen, financiers, businessmen, intellectuals and literati. They did so in medieval Spain. They did so again as Enlightenment dawned. They contributed an astonishing number of the makers of the modern mind: Spinoza, Marx, Freud, Einstein, Proust, Kafka, Canetti, Mahler, Schoenberg, Wittgenstein, Levi-Strauss, Adorno, Isaiah Berlin, Chomsky, Pissarro, Chagall, Soutine, Modigliani. Jews revolutionised thought, art, politics, the cinema. They pioneered in disciplines from music to medicine. Numerically insignificant, they won a remarkable percentage of Nobel prizes. In Britain they have provided, out of all proportion to their numbers, Cabinet ministers and Masters of Oxbridge colleges.

When the gates were closed and the Jewish mind turned inward, its creative pulse hardly missed a beat as it directed its energies to Jewish law and piety and mystic speculation. In the darkest environments – France and Germany of the Crusades, the century after the expulsion from Spain, the benighted villages of eighteenth-century Eastern Europe – Jews carried with them a pillar of fire. Surrounded by poverty, ignorance and superstition, they sustained a life of literacy and religious scholarship. In *yeshivot* and Hasidic circles they penetrated the heavens. In Hamlet's phrase, their kingdom might be bounded by a nutshell, but they were kings of infinite space.

Wherever they went, the Jews carried a message whose content varied little through the ages and which constituted the core of the Jewish contribution to mankind. Through the Bible, they had learned that God and nature are radically distinct. Jews had been the first to distinguish faith from myth and place it instead on the foundations of ethics. They taught that human beings have freewill and therefore moral choice and responsibility. They believed that human life is sacred, that the individual is made in 'the image of God', that justice is a supreme value, and that right is distinct from might. They insisted that no human power is beyond reproach and that a prophet may criticise a king. They taught that freedom is the touchstone of civilisation and that God Himself redeems slaves. Against every other theory of time, they maintained that history has meaning and is the stage on which man encounters God. They had faith that humanity, though corrupt, is redeemable and that our destination is the messianic age. Against every premature consolation, they taught that salvation lies not in the past but in the future. As long as violence and injustice reign, the messianic age is not yet.

Through its daughter religions, Christianity and Islam, Judaism taught monotheism to the world, and with it the supremacy of ethics. To quote Paul Johnson again:

All the great conceptual discoveries of the intellect seem obvious and inescapable once they have been revealed, but it requires a special genius to formulate them for the first time. The Jews had this gift. To them we owe the idea of equality before the law, both divine and human; of the sanctity of life and the dignity of the human person; of the individual conscience and so of personal redemption; of the collective conscience and so of social responsibility; of peace as an abstract ideal and love as the foundation of justice, and many items which constitute the basic moral furniture of the human mind. Without the Jews it might have been a much emptier place.

Western civilisation owes its character to two decisive influences,

Athens and Jerusalem, the homes respectively of Greek reason and Jewish revelation, of Greek aesthetics and Jewish ethics. Without this tiny people, the Jews – seldom more and often less than half a per cent of the population of the world – human history would have run a different course.

HEIRS TO ETERNITY

Jews did more than survive under seemingly impossible circumstances. They maintained their distinctiveness against every inducement – sometimes benign, often brutal – to assimilate or convert. To every crisis they responded with renewal. Heirs to one of the world's oldest faiths, they remained perennially young, creative, challenging, revolutionary. In each generation they embellished their ancient faith with new customs and interpretations and made it gleam as if it had just been given. Whenever the opportunity arose they enriched the life of the larger society in which they lived. Through thirty-seven long and difficult centuries they remained faithful to the mandate given by God to Abraham in the first words of covenantal history: 'Through you shall all the families of the earth be blessed.'

And we are their heirs. Was there ever a more challenging proposition that this? Milton Himmelfarb once wrote: 'Each Jew knows how thoroughly ordinary he is; yet taken together, we seem caught up in things great and inexplicable.' He was right. As individuals, there is nothing remarkable about Jews. There have been many theories, Jewish and non-Jewish, which attribute to us an innate genius, a racial gift, a genetic endowment, a mystic difference. None is convincing. Removed from our traditions, our past, our way of life and our community, within three generations or less we merge into the wider landscape and become invisible. Individually we are ordinary. Collectively we become something else.

For that reason we always set as our first and highest goal the transmission of identity across the generations. A Jewish child knew that he or she was something special, that he or she was 'caught up in things great and inexplicable'. For each of us, surely, there was such a childhood moment whose significance we only realised many years later. Was it the first *seder* at which we asked the four questions and perhaps, even then, dimly sensed the huge history of which we were the latest chapter? Was it when we began to learn Hebrew and translate verses from the Bible and slowly realised that a single ancestral chain linked us to Abraham and Sarah? Was it when we first attended synagogue and heard the sad, haunting melodies which seemed to speak of faraway sufferings and an unfathomable faith? Whenever it was, however it happened, at that moment we stumbled inadvertently on the great secret of Jewish existence: that though we might not be born great or achieve greatness, our history thrusts greatness upon us. We are more than individuals. We are part of a collective history and destiny, perhaps the strangest and most miraculous the world has ever known. That is our inheritance, and the most important thing we can do is to hand it on to our children.

THE BREAKING CHAIN

That is what Jews did for thousands of years. *And that is what we are failing to do now*. With a speed and suddenness that has caught us unawares, the chain of Jewish continuity is breaking. In Britain, America, and throughout most of the diaspora, one young Jew in every two is deciding not to marry another Jew and have Jewish children.

I tremble as I write these words, and yet I must do so again: In Britain, America, and throughout most of the diaspora, one young Jew in every two is deciding not to marry another Jew and have Jewish children. In any age this would be an unspeakable tragedy. There were times – fifteenth-century Spain was one – when under terror and the threat of death Jews converted to Christianity. There were other times – eighteenth-century Germany and nineteenth-century Russia – when anti-Jewish prejudice was such that Jews chose assimilation, in Heinrich Heine's famous phrase, as their 'entrance ticket to European culture'. But today in countries where intermarriage is at its highest, there is no terror or threat. No avenues are closed. On the contrary, Jews in Britain and America are the best educated, most successful and most upwardly mobile of any religious or ethnic group. And yet Jews are choosing not to hand on their inheritance to their chidren.

In any age this would be a tragedy. In ours it is worse. For we have lived through the century in which, between 1941 and 1945, one third of the Jewish people died. Eighty per cent of European Jewry was murdered. More than one million Jewish children were shot, gassed or buried alive. To this day we do not, nor perhaps to the end of time will we, understand the Holocaust. But there is one thing which every Jew understands, best summed up in the words of Emil Fackenheim, that we must not hand Hitler 'a posthumous victory'. What greater posthumous victory can we give the enemies of Jewry than, in the space of the next generation, to cease to be Jews?

That is a question from the heart of darkness. But in the opposite direction there is a question from the core of light. For nearly two thousand years our ancestors prayed for the freedom to live without persecution as Jews. Since the collapse of the Bar Kochba rebellion and the start of a seemingless endless exile, they prayed that one day they would be gathered in to their land. At the two climaxes of the Jewish year, at the Pesach *seder* and at the end of Yom Kippur, they yearned for 'Next year in Jerusalem'. In our time, these prayers have been answered. In Britain and America, Jews are free to live as Jews and are respected when they do. In Israel, ancient prophecies have come true. After nineteen hundred years of wandering, Jews have a home and a sovereign state. Jerusalem has been reunited and rebuilt. Hebrew, the ancient language of the Bible, has become again the living language of Jewish speech. There is no precedent in all of human history for this renaissance and return. How can it be that, at the very time when the hopes that drove us for centuries have become reality, Jews are turning their backs on hope and reality alike and ceasing to be Jews?

These are profound questions which cannot be fully answered here. In this book, I confine myself to manageable themes. What is happening to the contemporary diaspora, in which Anglo-Jewry is no exception to the rule? Why is it happening? And what, as a community, can we do to reverse the trend? These are straightforward, quantifiable and practical issues. Underlying them, though, is one fundamental proposition, the proposition I have argued here.

If we are Jews it is because our ancestors were Jews and because they braved much and sacrificed more to ensure that their children would be Jews. Can we do less? In the only verse in the entire Bible which explains why God chose Abraham – and thus Israel, and therefore us – we read: 'For I have chosen him so that he will command his children and his household after him to keep the way of the Lord by doing what is right and just.' Abraham was chosen because he would hand his way of life on to future generations. Ever afterward, until modern times, his descendants did likewise. Can we do otherwise?

The miracle of Jewish continuity is too precious for us to let it fail. Nor need it fail. I began this chapter with the oldest surviving words written by non-Jews about Jews. They were an obituary. 'Israel is laid waste: his seed is not.' In one form or another those words have been pronounced many times, not only by Merneptah of Egypt and Mesha of Moab, but by a succession of tyrants from Haman to Hitler. More than three thousand years later, the people Israel lives. It is not that we were unscarred by our enemies. We were afflicted and wounded, and after the Holocaust, we limp. Yet, the Jewish will to live and confer Jewish life upon our children proved stronger than the greatest empire. It is this that is now in danger, as never before.

2
The Crisis

In November 1992 the General Assembly of the Council of Jewish Federations met in New York. The agenda was dominated by one theme: *continuity*. The Strategic Planning Committee of the UJA-Federation of New York delivered a report on the future prospects of the Jewish community. It presented its conclusions in the form of an imaginary article which might well be published in the *New York Times* forty years from now. The article began:

New York, June 2, 2032. It was a time for memories and tears yesterday as the United Jewish Federation of New York formally ceased operations. The Federation, once known as UJA-Jewish Federation of New York, and its predecessor organizations had once served a community of more than 2 million Jews. Now that the Jewish community numbers fewer than 200,000 persons...

The article was prompted by the hard demographic facts that, contrary to the optimistic predictions of the 1980s that American Jewry was surviving, even reviving, it was in fact disappearing at an unprecedented rate. Outmarriage was at an all-time high, up a thousand per cent on the figures of thirty years previously. The American Jewish community now included 2.1 million non-Jewish spouses and children of mixed marriages. Of the 3.2 million Jewish households, only 1.8 million – barely more than a half – consisted of Jews living exclusively with other Jews.

The November 1992 issue of *The Jerusalem Report* carried on its front cover the headline 'America's Vanishing Jews: Intermarriage Threatens the World's Largest Community'. It told the story of the devastating statistics of the recent National Jewish Population Survey and traced some of its consequences. Despite the unique power of American Jewry's fund-raising machine, money raised by the United Jewish Appeal has fallen consistently in real terms since the 1970s. Leading Jewish organisations such as B'nai B'rith have suffered dramatic falls in membership and income. The conclusion is inescapable. American Jewry is disappearing faster than perhaps any leading community since the Ten Lost Tribes.

In one respect, though, American Jewry is in a better condition than Anglo-Jewry. The Hasidic master, Rabbi Henoch of Alexander, said: 'The greatest exile is not to know that you are in exile.' Likewise, the greatest crisis is not to know that you are in crisis. That is the Anglo-Jewish situation.

About ten years ago the *Sunday Times* published a front page article about the sharp and dramatic fall in synagogue marriages. The news was treated as an item of national interest. By contrast, the Jewish community ignored it almost completely. There was no shock-wave, no debate, no discussion, no further research commissioned into the dimensions of the problem and its causes.

For the past few years the Board of Deputies Community Research Unit has been compiling yearly statistics on synagogue marriages within Anglo-Jewry. In 1991 the Unit completed a study which showed that the number of first marriages had fallen to significantly less than *half* of the figure at which it should stand if all Jews in Britain reaching marriageable age were marrying in a synagogue. The implication is simple. More than a half of young Jews are not marrying other Jews, or not marrying, or not celebrating their marriages under Jewish auspices. The loss cannot be explained in terms of *aliyah*, Jews leaving Britain for Israel. The number doing so is small, and is compensated for by foreign-born Jews marrying in Britain. Instead, the statistic spells disaffiliation and decline. Again there has been no furore, no debate, no response. Appeals by the Community Research Unit for additional resources to fund further research to understand what is happening to young Jews have gone unheeded.

The research that created the storm in America – the Council of Jewish Federation's 1990 National Jewish Population Survey – was conducted by an outstanding demographer, Dr Barry Kosmin. Dr Kosmin heads the most sophisticated social research department in the diaspora, the North American Jewish Data Bank. The irony is that until a few years ago Dr Kosmin, himself an Anglo-Jew, worked for the British Jewish community – for the Board of Deputies Community Research Unit. We had in London a Jewish social scientist of world ranking, whose work until the late 1980s was dedicated to providing Anglo-Jewry with information about itself. Eventually, he was driven to leave by the sheer indifference to his work. He had produced groundbreaking studies such as *Jewish Identity in an Anglo-Jewish Community* (the 'Redbridge Report') and (with Professor Stanley Waterman) *British Jewry in the '80s*. These reports contained several striking and potentially controversial findings that had significant implications for communal planning. But no one was listening. So he left.

Professor Daniel Elazar of Bar Ilan University, the Jerusalem Institute and a founder of the Jerusalem Institute of Public Affairs, was driven to this conclusion in a recent handbook of world Jewry: 'By and large, the powers that be in British Jewry are content with the status quo and do not seek change. At most they bemoan the decline of British Jewry but, like their British peers, do little to try to alter their state.' American Jewry knows it faces a crisis of continuity. We do not, and *that is the crisis.*

AGAINST DESPAIR

What are the facts and dimensions of the problem? Because American Jewry has a wealth of data while Anglo-Jewry has little, many of the figures quoted here are drawn from the United States. America, it is often said, is a different case. But this is only partially true. Where American Jewry is today, Anglo-Jewry is in danger of being tomorrow. Indeed, the trends now being uncovered in the United States characterise the diaspora as a whole, as a host of demographic studies has shown. The American situation, then, is crucial to an understanding of our own. For the challenge facing Anglo-Jewry today is the same as that of all diaspora communities: creating Jewish continuity in an age of radical discontinuity.

Before proceeding, a warning is necessary. The portrait sketched below is bleak and there is a danger that it may lead to despair. Despair is not a Jewish emotion. *Od lo avda tikvatenu*: our hope, we say, has never been destroyed. For there is a Jewish way of telling the story of our situation. The Mishnah instructs us, *matchil bignut umesayem beshevach*, to 'begin with the bad news and end with the good'. That is how we tell the story of the exodus on Pesach and that is how we have always told the narrative of Jewish history. We begin with exile and end with redemption. We start with catastrophe and culminate with hope. The rabbis said: 'Whenever you find the phrase "and it *came* to pass", this is always a sign of suffering. Whenever you find the phrase "and it *shall come* to pass", this is always a sign of joy.' The past might be cause for lamentation, but the future still holds its promise. The reason lies deep in Jewish consciousness. As Rabbi Zvi Hirsch Chajes explains, one of our most profound beliefs is that there is meaning in history. Providence is interwoven in our lives. What happens is not chance but a chapter in the complex script of the covenant which leads, mysteriously but assuredly, to our redemption. Crisis in Jewish history has always led to renewal, not despair. So it must be now. With this preface, we can now turn to the bad news.

THE MISSING CHILDREN

The most obvious test of a people's numerical strength is its birth-rate. By this measure, diaspora Jewry has been in decline for over a century. With few exceptions in few countries, Jews exhibit the lowest birth-rates of any religious or ethnic group.

In the United States, for example, Jews have had a lower rate of fertility than Catholics or Protestants in every decade of the twentieth century. At one time, in the 1970s, this had fallen to an average of 1.2 children per childbearing couple, far below the population replacement figure of 2.1. The rate has since risen. But it still heralds a declining and ageing Jewish population and one that is consistently shrinking in absolute terms and even more so relative to other population groups. In Anglo-Jewry similar findings have emerged. In his Redbridge survey, Dr Barry Kosmin found that in both 1967 and 1977, Redbridge Jews were 20 per cent below the fertility rate of Britain as a whole.

Jews are either marrying late or not marrying or, once marrying, are not having children in the numbers that other groups do. Analysts have been unable to come up with a simple explanation of why this is so, and perhaps there is no single cause. What we can say with some certainty, however, is that it is an effect of emancipation. Demographic studies of Europe in the nineteenth and early twentieth centuries have shown that wherever and whenever Jews emerged into an open society their birth-rates abruptly changed from above to below the national average.

INTERMARRIAGE

Even had there been no outmarriage, therefore, we would today be concerned about the state of Jewish survival. Nevertheless, the single most dramatic change in recent years has been in outmarriage itself. This has been a problem of Jewish life since the very beginning of the covenant. Abraham was concerned that Isaac should not marry into the local Canaanite population. Isaac and Rebekah were distressed when their son Esau married two Hittite women. Moses delivered warnings against intermarriage. Ezra and Nehemiah, returning to Israel after the

Babylonian exile, instituted drastic measures against those who had been 'unfaithful to our God by marrying foreign women from the peoples around us'. The rabbis of Mishnaic times enacted protective decrees against behaviour that might lead to outmarriage. So the problem is not new. But its dimensions are.

In America, for example, intermarriage was estimated in the 1920s at no more than one per cent. A study in 1944 yielded a figure of 2.6 per cent. Until the 1960s the rate remained at or below six per cent. The turning point came in the 1960s. In the first half of that decade the rate of intermarriage jumped to 17.4 per cent, and by 1971 it had risen to 31.7 per cent. Even then, however, the nature of what was happening was not fully appreciated, and it took the 1990 National Jewish Population Survey to send shock-waves through American Jewry. What the survey showed was that the rate had risen to 57 per cent. More than one Jew in two was marrying out. The speed at which this has happened has been overwhelming. From six per cent in 1960 to 57 per cent in the late 1980s means that *the intermarriage rate has risen almost ten times in less than thirty years.* The great chain of Jewish continuity, stretching back some four thousand years, is in danger of breaking in a single generation.

Though the latest figures have sent a shock-wave through American Jewry, they merely confirm what demographers have known for some time. Neil Sandberg, for example, had shown some years ago that intermarriage in Los Angeles rose from 11.6 per cent among first generation Americans to 43.5 per cent among the fourth generation. A study of Denver Jewry in the early 1980s showed that the percentage of intermarried households rose from 53 per cent among those aged 30–39 to 72 per cent among those aged 18–29. In Phoenix, the parallel figures were 43 per cent and 72 per cent. Once intermarriage gains a hold in a community, its increase is rapid and seemingly inexorable. Over three generations – Jewish immigrants and their children and grandchildren – Jewish identity can be sustained. In the fourth generation, ties of kinship and ethnicity weaken and mixed marriage soars.

No less significantly, the stigma traditionally attaching to outmarriage has almost entirely disappeared. *Only one-fifth of young American Jews declared themselves opposed in principle to mixed marriage, and only six per cent strongly so.* The importance of this statistic is that in the area of group continuity, attitudes are no less significant than behaviour. In a completely open society, where Jewish identity is a matter of voluntary commitment and choice, the fact that only a tiny minority of Jews indicate that they are opposed to an act that will almost certainly mean that their grandchildren will not be Jewish must be a matter for the gravest concern.

When I was last in America, in 1989, my eye was caught by a story on the front page of the *New York Times*. It was headed 'The Assimilating Bagel', and the tale it told was this. A bagel was once a hard, round roll with a large hole in the centre. It was a Jewish delicacy which you ate with cream cheese or smoked salmon and temporarily forgot the troubles of the world. But according to the *New York Times* the bagel was subtly changing. Its crust was getting softer. The hole was getting smaller. Little by little, the bagel was assimilating into a bun. For 'bagel' read 'Jewry' and the metaphor is clear. Jewish identity in America is vanishing with frightening, unprecedented speed.

ANGLO-JEWRY

In Britain, we lack this kind of exhaustive, detailed research. None the less, for some years there has been a disturbing fall in the number of marriages recorded in British synagogues.

Before the Second World War the number of Anglo-Jewish marriages was around three thousand a year. The figure dipped during the war and rose thereafter, but between the mid-1950s and the 1970s it fell precipitously to around fifteen hundred per annum. By the 1980s it had fallen further to some one thousand per annum. Community marriage rates have been consistently less than half the national rates since the mid-1950s. They have now reached the critical position where they represent less than one half of Jews of marriageable age, suggesting that *more than half of young Jews are not marrying, are marrying out, or are leaving the community in some other way.*

This trend is confirmed by a recently published survey (reported in the *Jewish Chronicle*, 24 September 1993) conducted by Jewish Care. *Fifty-three per cent of Jewish men between the ages of twenty and thirty-five said that they had married, or would consider marrying, someone of another religion.* This figure is all the more striking given that those questioned had attended a debate on Jewish life, in aid of a Jewish charity, thereby signalling some interest and commitment. Amongst the uncommitted, the figure is almost certain to be higher. This suggests that resistance to intermarriage has collapsed in Anglo-Jewry just as it has in America.

In fact, the situation is worse. An estimated three hundred *gittin* (religious divorces) are currently issued each year by British rabbinic courts. On the basis of this figure, Rabbi Dr Julian Shindler has calculated that the ratio of divorces to marriages in Anglo-Jewry has risen to approximately three in ten. If we were to add even a small conjectural figure for marriages terminated civilly but not religiously, the true rate may be nearer one in three. Therefore, we may conclude that Jews are not marrying other Jews, and if they do, they are likely to marry late and have few children. Even then, on current trends, one in three marriages will collapse. The Jewish family, for millennia the crucible of continuity, is fissuring and beginning to fail.

These trends, common to both Britain and America, signal a crisis in Jewish continuity. Whether we speak halakhically, biologically or culturally, Jewish identity has always been passed on through the family. In Israel it is supported in the public domain by a Jewish state, society and culture. In the diaspora, on the other hand, it is either sustained in the framework of marriage, parenthood and a Jewish home, or it disintegrates. Every indication suggests that for many, even most, young Jews, Jewish identity is not being sustained.

Kosmin's expert assessment is this: 'In historical terms, the change in the demography of the Jewish people in the twentieth century is not only unparalleled but catastrophic. ... Unless the erosion of Jewish numbers can be halted, the Jews are destined for the future of an endangered species.'

AN IDENTIFIABLE JEWISH COMMUNITY?

One result of the rise in outmarriage is an unprecedented confusion of Jewish identity. Despite the fact that it ignored the profound differences between Orthodox, Conservative and Reform Judaism and their conflicting approaches to conversion and Jewish status, the 1990 National Jewish Population Survey was forced to abandon the concept of a single measure of the Jewish population. Its authors found that they could quantify American Jewry only by dividing it into the following categories:

– Born Jews, Religion Judaism
– Jews by choice (converts of all denominations)
– Jews by religion (the sum of the previous two categories)
– Born Jews with no religion (secular Jews)
– Born or raised Jewish, converted out

- Adults of Jewish parentage with other current religion (usually children of a mixed marriage with one Jewish parent, who have been raised as Christians)
- Children under 18 being raised with other current religion.

The survey showed a 'core Jewish population' of 4.2 million. Around the core was a variety of 'marginal' groups: 1.1 million secular Jews, 185,000 converts, and 1,325,000 Jews who, whether through conversion or upbringing, today identify themselves as adherents of another religion, usually Christianity. Considered in their own right, these are disturbing figures. Considered in the light of current trends, they are portents of much worse to come.

THE END OF OPTIMISM

In the mid-1980s, as demographers began to sound the alarm, there was determined resistance by a group of American intellectuals who argued that the Jewish community was not disintegrating. It was merely in a state of transformation. Mixed marriage was not a catastrophe. It might even prove to be a blessing in disguise.

Their argument was this. There had been times in the past – particularly in the pre-Christian era – when Judaism had been an actively missionary faith. It had sought converts. It could do so again. After all, Judaism was an attractive option in a pluralistic society. Jewishness was no longer what Heinrich Heine had once called it: 'not a religion but a misfortune'. On the contrary, Jews were now the most educated and affluent group in America. Moreover, American Reform Judaism had begun a campaign to ease the path of entry into the Jewish fold. It had eased the standards for conversion and had even declared that it would consider Jewish, without the need for conversion, the child of a non-Jewish mother and a Jewish father. Charles Silberman set out the equation in his much discussed book, *A Certain People*: 'If half the children of intermarriages are raised as Jews, there will be no net reduction in the number of Jews, no matter how high the inter-marriage rate is.'

Rarely has an illusion been more quickly dispelled. We now know that this optimism was massively misplaced. The latest figures show that among the 57 per cent of Jews who marry out, in only five per cent of cases does the non-Jewish partner convert to Judaism. In the remaining 52 per cent of cases the partner retains his or her original religion. Within these mixed marriages, only 28 per cent of children are raised as Jews; 41 per cent are raised as Christians; 31 per cent are raised without religion at all.

There is, in short, no solace in these figures. Jews in America are failing to sustain themselves as a distinctive group at anything like previous numerical levels. They have too few children. More than half of them marry out. Even when they marry other Jews, the partnership is increasingly likely to end in divorce, and second marriages are even more likely to be outmarriages. The prospect that mixed marriage might result in a net gain for the Jewish community has disappeared. Non-Jewish partners are disinclined to convert, and in three-quarters of mixed marriages the children are not brought up as Jews.

In an age of shifting religious affiliations, Judaism has been the loser. The outflow of Jews to other religions has been vastly greater than the inflow through conversion, despite the efforts of liberal denominations to engage in active proselytisation and open the gates of admission more widely than Jews have ever done before. The sobering fact is that in the United States – the diaspora community for which we have the most accurate and reliable demographic evidence – *for every non-Jew who has become a Jew even by the most lenient standards, there are between seven and eight Jews who have become adherents of other religions and six who profess to no faith at all.*

Nor is our own community safe from such a fate. As I have noted already, British Jewry, estimated at 450,000 in the 1950s, is today reckoned to number some 300,000. This represents *the loss of more than ten Jews a day, every day, for forty years.* Of these, at most a fifth have left for Israel. The rest have disaffiliated and disappeared from the Jewish map.

AN UNFOLDING TRAGEDY

These are the facts, and they are very bad news. In the century of the Holocaust, they are nothing short of tragic. After the Shoah, one phrase came to encapsulate the collective response of world Jewry: 'Never again.' Never again would we stand by defenceless as Jews were dying because they were Jews. Yet, albeit in a radically different form, it *is* happening again. Admittedly, it is not Jews who are dying. But it is no less significant from the perspective of Jewish continuity. Judaism and Jewish identity are dying: that which made us Jews and gave shape and meaning to our lives.

Every nation that suffered casualties during the Second World War has since repopulated itself. Except the Jewish people. For every Jewish child who perished in the Holocaust there is a child today who could have been enjoying a free and secure Jewish identity, but is not, because its parents have divorced, or because one of its parents is not Jewish, or because it has no understanding or knowledge of what it is to be a Jew.

Jews are not dying, but Judaism and Jewish identity are. There is no moral comparison between these phenomena and none is intended. Nevertheless, in one respect the effect is the same. Jewish survival is once more in doubt. The catastrophe is spiritual and cultural, not physical. It is passive, not active. It is motivated by no malign intentions. However, it has consequences no less significant for the course of Jewish history. A people once known for its loyalty to a unique destiny is vanishing into oblivion. A nation whose seemingly infinite capacity for survival excited the astonishment of historians is losing its will to survive.

To put the comparison a different way: until the twentieth century, despite the terrible suffering experienced by Jews, none of their enemies believed that they had no right to live. From time to time, however, they did believe that they had no right to live *as Jews*. Consider three such moments.

The book of Esther describes the first edict of genocide, Haman's order 'to destroy, kill and annihilate all the Jews, young and old, women and little children, on a single day'. But, as the narrative makes clear, Haman would have harboured no enmity towards the Jews had they been prepared to do one thing: to bow down. Mordechai refused, as Jews have consistently refused to prostrate themselves before the idols of their time. Haman thus discovered a feature of Jewish life which has been, before and since, the touchstone of our identity. Jews are a people apart. 'There is,' as he told the king, 'a certain people dispersed and scattered among the peoples in all the provinces of your kingdom who keep themselves separate.' That was the prelude to genocide: not that Jews existed, but that Jews *persisted as Jews*, as a 'certain people' who, despite their dispersion, maintained their identity. *When over half of young Jews decide not to marry Jews and have Jewish children, we grant Haman a posthumous victory.*

On 31 March 1492, Ferdinand and Isabella of Spain decreed the expulsion of the Jews from their lands. It was the most traumatic event of the Jewish middle ages. Jews had been expelled from other countries before, notably from England in 1290. But Spain had been the setting for medieval Jewry's golden age. During its periods of relative liberalism, Jews had risen to take their place among the leading statesmen, poets, scientists, philosophers, doctors, traders and financiers of the time. Spanish Jewry had glittered in the brief sunshine, and when the storm of expulsion overwhelmed them, the shock-waves were felt throughout the Jewish world for centuries. Yet the decree was not directed against Jews as such. It was directed against Jews who remained Jews. It was not racial but religious in intent. Jews were offered a choice: convert to Christianity and stay, or remain Jewish and leave. *Today, when four-fifths of young American Jews are not against marrying out of the faith, we grant Queen Isabella of Spain a posthumous victory.*

Martin Luther (1483–1546) the leader of the Protestant Reformation in Germany, was one of Jewry's most virulent opponents. In *Concerning the Jews and their Lies* (1543) he set out a programme that was to be taken up in precise detail by the Nazis four centuries later: synagogues were to be burned, Jewish property seized, homes destroyed and Jews 'put under one roof or in a stable like gypsies'. It was, writes Paul Johnson, 'the first work of modern anti-Semitism and a giant step forward on the road to the Holocaust'. But Luther was not originally an antisemite. On the contrary, he believed that Jews would welcome his break with the Papacy, and would voluntarily convert *en masse* to his new Christianity. In 1523 he had written: 'I hope that if the Jews are treated friendly and are instructed kindly through the Bible many of them will become real Christians. ... I would advise and beg everybody to deal kindly with the Jews and to instruct them in the Scriptures; in such a case we could expect them to come over to us.' Luther's principle in those early days was that Jews would be converted by kindness. It was only anti-Jewish hostility that had kept them from assimilating to the majority. *In the century of the Holocaust we are granting Luther an astonishing posthumous victory.*

That we should allow millennia of Jewish continuity to come to an end for one Jew in two is unthinkable. What would become of every sacrifice our ancestors made in order to live as Jews and raise children as Jews? What would become of that extraordinary history of courage and persistence that so astounded Pascal and Nietzsche? What would become of the meaning of the covenant? If the past lays any obligation on us at all, it is that we cannot let the Jewish story end this way, in ignominious anticlimax. The minority of Jews who defected in the past did so under overwhelming pressure, in the face of threat and persecution, hatred and exclusion. Post-biblical history contains no precedent for the mass disappearance of Jews for no other reason than a loss of the will to hand our identity on to our children.

COUNTING JEWS

The news is bad. But the test of a people's spirit lies in how it responds to bad news. If we are to respond Jewishly we must rule out *ab initio* two reactions: denial and despair. Denial argues that there is nothing to worry about. Despair says that there is nothing we can do. Against this, faith is the courage to face facts, however painful, without losing hope. The facts *are* painful. Our children are choosing, in unprecedented numbers, not to have Jewish children. How then should we respond?

The Torah contains a remarkable perspective on demography. In the book of Exodus, God tells Moses: 'When you take a census of the Israelites to count them, each one must pay the Lord a ransom for his life at the time he is counted. Then no plague will come on them when you number them.'

In other words, *it is hazardous to count Jews*. Elsewhere, in the second book of Samuel and the first book of Chronicles, we read of how King David ignored the advice of his chief of staff Yoav, and took a census of Israel with disastrous consequences.

Why is it hazardous to count Jews? Our tradition records many explanations. But Jewish history suggests a simple answer. At most times in our history we have been a tiny people. Despite the promises which we believe will one day be fulfilled – that the descendants of Abraham and Sarah would be as many as the stars of the sky, the dust of the earth and the sand of the sea shore – thus far we have been one of the world's smallest peoples.

By the end of the book of Genesis the people of Israel numbered no more than seventy individuals. At the end of his life, Moses declared to the now much more numerous nation in the wilderness: 'The Lord did not set his affection on you and choose you because you were more numerous than other peoples, for you are the fewest of all peoples.' From then on, Israel remained a small country ranged against great empires: Assyria, Babylon, Persia, Greece and Rome. At almost no time in history has the people Israel been a numerically significant population. This was true even when it was a sovereign power in its own land. Still more was it true when it was a scattered and exiled diaspora.

The Crisis

Historians have estimated that between the fall of the second Temple in 70 CE and the seventeenth century, the Jewish population never rose above 1.5 million. At times, as in the wake of the Spanish expulsion, it fell to below a million. Jewry increased significantly only between 1800 and 1939, when it grew from two million to 16.6 million. At no time in the last nineteen hundred years have Jews constituted even one per cent of the population of the world.

Nevertheless, Jews did more than survive. Throughout history we have been at the epicentre of world history. In periods of toleration, Jews rose with astonishing speed to the forefront of human achievement. The Judaic heritage shaped and continues to shape Western civilisation. As a result, Jews could rarely be ignored. From earliest times to the present day, both the friends and the enemies of the Jews have attributed us to an influence far beyond our numbers. Demographically, we have been grasshoppers. In impact and influence we have been giants. Milton Himmelfarb put it graphically: 'The number of Jews in the world is smaller than a small statistical error in the Chinese census. Yet we remain bigger than our numbers. Big things seem to happen around us and to us.'

This has given rise to a most curious phenomenon. Recently, a research exercise was conducted in the United States in which people at random were asked to estimate the percentage of the American population that was Jewish. The average answer given was about 20 per cent. The true figure is two per cent. The experiment can be repeated with similar results almost anywhere that Jews live. We always seem to be many times more numerous than we actually are.

Why then is it hazardous to count Jews? Because when we take a census we are basing our strength on numbers. Jewish strength has never lain in numbers. When we count Jews there is a serious danger that we will become demoralised, realising that we are so few. When a people depends – as the Jewish people depends – on its spirit and sense of pride, demoralisation can be nothing short of catastrophic. It can lead to despair, and from despair to defeat.

King David was wrong to believe that his military strength depended on the size of his population, just as the State of Israel would be wrong to think likewise today. If military strength does not depend on numbers, still less does ethical or intellectual or religious strength. The inscription beneath the portrait of Jewish history still reads: 'Not by might nor by power, but by My spirit.'

What is troubling about present demographic trends in the diaspora is not the fact that there are fewer Jews and hence less Jewish influence and power. In the diaspora we have never depended on power, nor has our influence anything to do with numbers. What is troubling is the message the statistics are telling us about the state of the Jewish spirit. Never before have Jews felt so indifferent to their heritage that they were unconcerned to pass it on to their children. Once we state the problem in these terms we are already halfway to a solution. For what is born in the spirit can be cured in the spirit. And no people has had greater experience in sustaining the human spirit than the heirs of those who stood at Sinai.

The question therefore is this: what is the skill at which Jews proved themselves so adept in the past and which we seem to have lost in the present? What is the secret of Jewish continuity?

3
The Secret

In 1899, the great American novelist Mark Twain wrote an article about the Jews. It ended with these words:

If the statistics are right, the Jews constitute but one per cent of the human race. It suggests a nebulous, dim puff of star dust lost in the blaze of the Milky Way. Properly the Jew ought hardly to be heard of; but he is heard of, has always been heard of. He is as prominent on the planet as any other people, and his commercial importance is extravagantly out of proportion to the smallness of his bulk. His contributions to the world's greatest names in literature, science, art, music, finance, medicine and abstruse learning are also way out of proportion to the smallness of his numbers.

He has made a marvellous fight in this world, in all the ages; and has done it with his hands tied behind him. The Egyptian, the Babylonian, and the Persian rose, filled the planet with sound and splendour, then faded to dreamstuff and passed away; the Greek and the Roman followed, and made a vast noise, and they are gone; other peoples have sprung up and held their torch high for a time, but it burned out, and they sit in twilight now, or have vanished. The Jew saw them all, beat them all, and is now what he always was, exhibiting no decadence, no infirmities of age, no weakening of his parts, no slowing of his energies, no dulling of his alert and aggressive mind. All things are mortal but the Jew; all other forces pass, but he remains. What is the secret of his immortality?

It is a marvellous tribute, but it ends with a question, the right question. What *is* the secret of Jewish survival? No ordinary answer will suffice, because Jewish history has been altogether extraordinary. Jews remained a distinctive nation without land, power, territory or a shared culture. They were dispersed and almost everywhere a minority. For the most part they refused active efforts to convert them, and they resisted the passive pull of assimilation. No other people has kept its identity intact for so long in such circumstances. How then did they do so?

Faith suggests an answer. At Sinai, Israel and God entered into a solemn and mutually binding pledge: the covenant. Israel would dedicate itself to God. God, in turn, would protect Israel. The Jewish people would exist, in Jeremiah's words, as long as the sun and the stars shone and the waves roared in the sea. Israel would be God's witnesses, and their eternity would mirror His. Jews survived for a simple reason. Interwoven in our history was something larger than history: Divine providence.

I believe this answer to be true. Nor has it appealed to believing Jews only. Secular and non-Jewish historians, too, have been moved to a sense of religious wonder as they have contemplated the enigma of our people. Heinrich Graetz, for example, in his conscious attempt to secularise Jewish self-understanding in his *History of the Jews* a century ago, was none the less prompted to write: 'The continuance of the Jewish race until the present day is a marvel not to be overlooked even by those who deny the existence of miracles, and who only see in the most astounding events, both natural and preternatural, the logical results of cause and effect.' So closely have the vicissitudes of Jewry mirrored the destiny laid out in the pages of the Bible that even the most hardened of sceptics has been forced into a temporary suspension of disbelief.

None the less, this answer cannot suffice – and not only for unbelievers, but for believers as well. A consistent thread runs through Jewish thought, from the Bible, through the sages, to the present day. Providence, we believe, is not a unilateral decree imposed by Heaven on humanity. God grants us freewill, and therefore no outcome in the affairs of man is certain in advance. The Bible does not contain *predictions*. It contains *prophecies*, which are very different things. A prophecy is a warning and the stark portrayal of a choice. This way lies blessing, that way lies curse, but there are always two roads and the choice is ours. If providence is written between the lines of Jewish history, as I believe it is, it is a providence that works through, and not independently of, the free decisions of Jews. The question therefore remains. Why did Jews, in difficult circumstances and for generation after generation, choose to continue to be Jews?

ANTISEMITISM AND JEWISH SURVIVAL

One answer was suggested by Spinoza. In order to understand it we should recall that Spinoza lived in an age still haunted by the Spanish expulsion. His ancestors had been Marranos, Jews who converted to Christianity in fifteenth-century Spain, but who remained Jews in secret. Theirs was the original crisis of identity. They were half Jews, half Christians, torn between two cultures and distrusted by both. By the time Spinoza reached intellectual maturity in the relatively liberal environment of seventeenth-century Amsterdam, he had become convinced that religion had done great harm to humanity. Reason promised more than revelation. There should be a separation of church and state. Public life should be secularised. Jews would then be free to rid themselves of the tragic Jewish fate without having to convert to another faith.

Given Spinoza's opposition to religion, he had to find a natural rather than a supernatural explanation for Jewish survival. His argument was striking and paradoxical. The Jews may have been threatened by antisemitism, but they had been preserved by it too. 'As to their continuance so long after dispersion and the loss of empire,' he wrote, 'there is nothing marvellous in it.' Jews kept themselves apart. Their laws were distinctive. They celebrated on special days and ate special foods. Indeed the whole code of Jewish law was a discipline of difference. The result was that they drew 'down upon themselves universal hate'. Yet, far from threatening Jewish existence, hostility reinforced it. 'That they have been preserved in great measure by Gentile hatred, experience demonstrates.'

Spinoza's argument cannot be lightly dismissed. Undoubtedly, antisemitisim has played a complex role in Jewish history. At times it threatened the very basis of Jewish survival: in the Crusades, the later expulsions, the Chmielnicki massacres of the seventeenth century, the pogroms of the nineteenth, and worst by far, the Shoah. At other times and in other ways, however, it formed a barrier against assimilation. It preserved a distance between Jews and their neighbours. Jews wishing to leave Judaism often found the doors barred, sometimes even after they had converted to Christianity. They were treated as outsiders, different, alien. Centuries later, assimilationists like Heinrich Heine and Max Nordau discovered the same thing. Heine eventually wrote: 'I am now hated by Jew and Christian alike. I am truly sorry that I permitted myself to be baptized.' Nordau described the Jew who 'has abandoned his specifically Jewish character, yet the nations do not accept him as part of their national communities. He flees from his Jewish fellow, because antisemitism has taught him, too, to be contemptuous of them, but his gentile compatriots repulse him as he attempts to associate with them.'

Antisemitism kept Jews apart. Indeed, the early rabbinic sages suggested something similar. Resh Lakish in the third century CE compared Israel to Noah's dove which found no rest. 'Had the dove found rest it would not have returned to the ark. Had Israel found rest among the nations, it too would not have returned to God.' Being too much at home in a non-Jewish culture could lead to a loss of Jewish identity. By contrast, persecution could lead to Jewish revival. Rabbi Joshua (early second century CE) argued that if Israel did not turn to God of their own accord, Heaven would send a king 'whose decrees will be as harsh as those of Haman' and Israel would then return. Earlier still, the prophet Ezekiel had warned 'You say: We want to be like the nations . . . But what you have in mind will never happen.' So prophets and sages saw the hand of providence in antisemitism. It reinforced from the outside what the Jews believed from within, that they were 'a people that dwells alone, not reckoned among the nations'.

None the less, this explanation is inadequate. Antisemitism sometimes prevented assimilation, but at other times it led to it. In fifteenth-century Spain, eighteenth-century Germany and nineteenth-century Russia, Jews abandoned Judaism to escape hostility. The fact that they failed did not prevent them from trying. Correspondingly, periods of religious tolerance can lead to a dilution of Jewish identity, but they can also promote revival. The Golden Age of Spain, and post-war America, witnessed not only Jewish defections but also a flowering of Jewish scholarship. There is no direct, linear relationship between Jewish continuity and the attitudes and policies of the non-Jewish environment. Mark Twain's question therefore remains: 'All things are mortal but the Jew . . . What is the secret of his immortality?'

A RELIGION OF CONTINUITY

The answer, I believe, is straightforward. *The secret of Jewish continuity is that no people has ever devoted more of its energies to continuity.* The focal point of Jewish life is the transmission of a heritage across the generations. Time and again in the Torah we are drawn to dramas of the next generation. Judaism's focus is its children. Abraham's first words to God are 'What can You give me, if I am without children?' Rachel says: 'Give me children, for without them it is as if I am dead.' To be a Jew is to be a link in the chain of generations. It is to be a child and then a parent, to receive and to hand on. Moses 'received the Torah at Sinai and handed it on . . .' and so must we. Judaism is *a religion of continuity.*

The Secret

We who have grown up with Judaism are so familiar with this idea that we take it as self-evident, but it is not. It is exceptional, even unique. The first command in the Torah is not *to believe*, but *to have children*. Abraham is chosen not because he is righteous (only Noah is described as that) but because 'he will instruct his children and his household after him'. On the brink of the exodus from Egypt, Moses does not spend time telling the Israelites about the land of milk and honey that awaits them across the Jordan. Instead, he instructs them about how they should teach future generations. Three times he returns to the theme: 'And when your children ask you . . .,' 'In days to come, when your son asks you . . .,' 'On that day you shall tell your son . . .' Not yet liberated, they are invited to become a nation of educators.

Thus, from the very outset, Judaism predicated its survival on education. Not education in the narrow, formal sense of the acquisition of knowledge but something altogether broader. Indeed, the word 'education' is wholly inadequate to describe Judaism's culture of study, meditation and debate, its absorption in texts, commentaries and counter-commentaries, its devotion to literacy and life-long learning. Descartes said: 'I think, therefore I am.' A Jew would have said: 'I learn, therefore I am.' If there is one *leitmotif*, one dominant theme linking the various periods of Jewish history it is enthronement of education as the sovereign Jewish value.

In one of the most famous verses in the Torah, Moses commands: 'You shall teach these things diligently to your children, speaking of them when you stay at home or when you travel on a journey, when you lie down and when you rise up.' The first Psalm describes the happy human being as one who 'studies Torah day and night'. In an astonishing commentary on rabbinic priorities, the fourth-century sage Rava, seeing another scholar prolonging his prayers when he might have been studying, said: 'Such people forsake eternal life and occupy themselves instead with temporal life.' The rabbis said: 'Greater is an illegitimate scholar than an ignorant high priest.'

The central, burning, incandescent passion of Jews was study. Their citadels were schools. Their religious leaders were sages: the word *rabbi* does not mean priest or holy man but *teacher*. Even when they were racked by poverty, they ensured that their children were educated. In twelfth-century France a Christian scholar noted: 'A Jew, however poor, if he has ten sons, will put them all to letters, not for gain as the Christians do, but for the understanding of God's law – and not only his sons but his daughters too.' In the *shtetl* (small township) of Eastern Europe, learning conferred prestige, status, authority and respect. Men of wealth were honoured, but scholars were honoured more. It was they who occupied the seats of rank along the synagogue's eastern wall. In their study of the culture of the *shtetl*, *Life is with People*, Zborowski and Herzog describe the impact this made on the Jewish family:

The most important item in the family budget is the tuition fee that must be paid each term to the teacher of the younger boys' school. 'Parents will bend the sky to educate their son.' The mother, who has charge of household accounts, will cut the family food costs to the limit if necessary, in order to pay for her son's schooling. If the worst comes to the worst, she will pawn her cherished pearls in order to pay for the school term. The boy must study, the boy must become a good Jew – for her the two are synonymous.

The result was that *Jews knew*. They knew who they were and why. They knew their history. They knew their traditions. They knew where they came from and where their hearts belonged. They had a sense of identity and pride. They knew Abraham and Moses and Isaiah and Hillel and Akiva and Rashi and Maimonides, for they had studied their words and argued over their meaning. The Torah was the portable homeland of the Jew, and they knew its landscape, its mountains and valleys, better than they knew the local scenery outside their windows. Jerusalem lay in ruins, but they were familiar with its streets from the prophets and the Talmud and they walked in the golden city of the mind. Nowhere else was literacy, scholarship and high culture so widely diffused, so highly prized as among this people of the book. Paul Johnson describes traditional Jewish life as an 'ancient and highly efficient social machine for the production of intellectuals'. It was an aristocracy of the spirit and mind. Not everyone, said Maimonides, can be a priest or a king. But the crown of Torah – the greatest of all crowns – is available to all.

THE TRANSMISSION OF IDENTITY

Identity is a delicate thing. It is *reality internalised*, how we see ourselves in relation to the world around us. For most people at most times, identity is not a problem. It is provided by the surrounding culture and its institutions. For Jews, however, it *has* been a problem at most times and places throughout our history. The reason is simple. Jewish identity was *not* provided by the surrounding culture, for Jews were a minority in a non-Jewish environment. Most minorities eventually give up the uneven struggle of maintaining a separate identity. Based as it is on tradition, memory and habit, identity is weakened as these are eclipsed by adjustment to the ways of the majority. It takes time – several generations – for this to happen. But almost invariably it does.

Jews were different, for they saw their identity not as an accident of history – who they happened to be – but as a religious vocation – who they were called on to be. From the very outset they did not rest content with tradition, memory and habit, the legacy of the past. They *renewed and recreated* the past in each successive generation. A Jewish child, on Pesach, tasted the unleavened bread and bitter herbs of Egyptian slavery. On Sukkot he joined his ancestors in their tabernacles as they journeyed precariously through the desert. On Tisha be'Av he sat with the author of Lamentations and mourned the destruction of the Temple and the sufferings of his people through the ages. In the most vivid way, Jews handed on their memories to their children.

Not only their memories but their way of life. Since the days of Moses, Jews have lived distinctively according to the laws set forth in the Torah. Had this rested on habit alone it would have gradually disappeared once Jews were exiled and dispersed. But Jews were never content with habit. They believed not only in keeping the law but in studying it as well. Rabbinic Judaism is the only civilisation in which every citizen is expected not just to obey the law but *to become a lawyer*, a student and exponent of the law. Jews were – to use David Reisman's terms – not tradition-directed but *inner*-directed individuals. The 'thou shalts' and 'thou shalt nots' of the Torah were not an external code but an internalised discipline, part of identity itself. That is how Jews were able to hand on their way of life to their children.

Even this might not have sufficed were it not for one other thing. Perhaps the most precious heritage Jews gave their children was *hope*. From the outset, Israel has been a remarkably future-oriented people. The story of Abraham begins with the promise of a land, but by the end of the book of Genesis it has still not been fulfilled. The book of Exodus begins with the Israelites leaving Egypt and travelling towards the land of milk and honey, but by the end of Deuteronomy they have still not arrived. In contrast with almost every other faith, Judaism's golden age lies not in the past but in the future, just over the horizon.

As a result, at every moment of crisis – the Babylonian exile, the Roman destruction, the Spanish expulsion – prophets, sages and mystics were able to rescue a people from despair by messianic intimations. Jews remembered their future as actively as they recalled their past. They prayed towards Jerusalem and mentioned it constantly because they knew it would one day be rebuilt, and they or their children would return. It is said that Napoleon, passing a synagogue on *Tisha be'Av* in 1806 and hearing sounds of weeping, asked what tragedy had just occurred. He was told: 'The destruction of Jerusalem seventeen centuries before.' He replied: 'A people that can mourn a city for so long will one day have it restored.' He was right. Jewish memory, because of its peculiar character, kept Jewish hope alive. This, too, led Jews to live for the future, which meant for and through their children.

IDENTITY IN THE DIASPORA

There is nothing inevitable about Jewish identity in the diaspora, and there never was. In Israel one is Jewish by living in a Jewish state, surrounded by a Jewish culture and Jewish institutions. But elsewhere, being Jewish means going against the grain, being counter-cultural. The most natural form of identity is to say, I belong to the here-and-now, to the people around me and the landscape I see every morning. Jews chose a more complex identity, and had they not done so they would have disappeared as Jews.

To be sure, since the days of Jeremiah they knew that their responsibility as citizens was to 'seek the peace of the city to which I have carried you into exile, and pray to the Lord for it, because if it prospers, you too will prosper'. So, whenever permitted, they entered into the life of Cairo and Cordova, Vilna and Vitebsk and left it enriched. But that was *where* they were, not *who* they were. Who they were was the very opposite of the here-and-now. It was a breathtaking identity spanning time and space, centuries and continents. Jews were defined by a network of relationships stretching back to the biblical past and forward to the messianic future, linked in a common destiny with Jews across the globe.

Diaspora Jewish identity was and is a matter of the mind, not the senses; of nurture, not nature. We live through what we learn. If we do not learn what it is to be a Jew, nothing in our environment, except antisemitism, will tell us. And antisemitism, while it may remind us that we are Jews, provides no reason for us to want our children to be Jewish. Jews survived, quite simply, because they devoted their best energies to education, their money to schools, their admiration to scholars, their spare hours to study, and their first concern to the tuition of their children. Their identity was constantly learned and relearned, enacted and reinforced, and passed on as a precious gift to the next generation. *The secret of Jewish continuity is that Jews cared about it. They created continuity by making the transmission of tradition their first duty and greatest joy.*

DEFYING DEATH

The rabbis of the Talmud had a way of communicating deep truths in the most simple language. They told the following story about King David. David, they said, was once overcome by thoughts of his own mortality and prayed to God to know how long he had to live. God replied that no one is allowed to know when he or she will die. 'Then let me know,' said David, 'on what day of the week I will die.' 'You will die,' said God, 'on Shabbat.' As soon as he heard this, King David resolved to spend every Shabbat in uninterrupted study.

The appointed day eventually came and the angel of death was sent to bring David to heaven. But 'learning did not cease from the mouth' of the king, and the angel was unable to lay hold of him. The angel knew it could not return to heaven empty-handed, so it devised a stratagem. It made a rustling noise in a tree in David's garden. The king went out to investigate, and started climbing a ladder. The ladder broke, and as David was falling, he paused for a moment from his learning. At that moment, the angel laid hold of him and King David died.

It is a subtle story. On the surface it is a simple example of *midrash aggadah*, one of those legends by which the sages fleshed out the bare bones of biblical narrative and made them come vividly alive. It is, however, much more than that. The sages, with their unique combination of simplicity and depth, were talking not just about King David but about themselves and the fate of the Jewish people.

They had lived through two military uprisings against Rome: the great rebellion of 66 CE, and the Bar Kochba rebellion of 132–135 CE. Both ended in disaster. As a result of the first, the Temple was destroyed. As a result of the second, the whole of Judea lay in ruins. Jerusalem was rebuilt as a Roman city, Aelia Capitolina, and Jews were refused entry on pain of death. Jews were profoundly affected by these two events. Not until the Warsaw Ghetto uprising in 1943 were they again to take up arms against their oppressors. The twin defeats of the first and second centuries were catastrophic and devastating. For as long as anyone could foresee, Jews would not be able to survive by military strength or defend themselves by conventional weapons. How then would they endure?

The sages gave a remarkable answer. The military arena was not the only, or even the most important, battle-field. Of far greater significance from the point of view of Jewish continuity was the arena of culture, civilisation and faith. The Maccabees, who had begun as pious rebels against the Seleucid Greeks and had won a stunning victory which we still commemorate on Hanukkah, eventually became allies of Rome and thus agents of the very Hellenisation they had once opposed. So it was possible to win battles and yet lose the war against assimilation. If so, might the reverse not also be true? Might it not be possible to lose battles and yet win the war of identity.

The great Jewish embodiment of military prowess was King David. But there was another David, author of the book of Psalms. Reflecting on their fate, the sages realised that it was this other David who was the enduring symbol of Jewish life, not waging war but engaged in what was to become the very pulse of Jewish life after the destruction of the second Temple: study. The talmudic story of King David and the angel of death is nothing less than a metaphor of the people of Israel and its fate. David stood for Israel, the warrior turned scholar. So long as he carried a book, not a sword, he would be immune. The sages, in a story calculated to appeal to children, propounded a sophisticated hypothesis: that *so long as their mouths did not desist from study, the angel of death would have no power over the Jewish people.* The Jews might have lost the battles with Rome but they would win the war against mortality. Individual Jews would live and die but the Jewish people would be eternal. With the hindsight of history, we now know that they were right.

Daniel Elazar, in his encyclopaedic survey of world Jewry, *People and Polity*, draws the simple conclusion:

> The history of the Jews has been a history of communities built around schools. They are the key institutions because they convey learning. Greek civilization survived for five hundred years after the Roman conquest of the Greek city-states, because the Greeks, like the Jews, had developed academies and they could live around those academies. When the academies failed, Greek civilization disappeared. The Jewish people has never allowed its academies to fail.

That is the secret of Jewish immortality.

4

Testing the Hypothesis

The hypothesis before us is this: that Jewish continuity in the diaspora depends on Jewish education. This, for most Jews at most times, was an item of faith. How shall we submit it to critical evaluation? What would constitute a test? There may be others, but let me suggest two: the test of history, and the test of the latest available research. First, history.

The Jewish people has survived. But at significant moments that survival lay in doubt. Catastrophe struck and there was no obvious route to a secure future. The prophets had declared that Israel would be an eternal people. But there were times when this seemed desperately unlikely. There were moments *when it might have been otherwise*. These critical junctures repay close attention. What saved the people and faith of Israel from the might-have-been of oblivion? Consider three such turning points.

The first came in the fifth century BCE. Several centuries earlier, the northern kingdom of Israel had been destroyed by the Assyrians. Its population was dispersed and rapidly assimilated into the neighbouring cultures. Ten of the twelve Israelite tribes disappeared from history. In 586 BCE the southern kingdom of Judah, comprising the two remaining tribes, was also overcome, this time by the Babylonians. The Temple was destroyed and the elite of the people taken into captivity. There they might also have disintegrated as a group, were it not for the insistent message of the prophets that hope was not lost.

Under Cyrus, king of Persia, a new and more benign regime took shape and some of the exiles were allowed to return. Eventually, under the leadership of Nehemiah, the statesman-governor, and Ezra, the priestly scribe, a Jewish renaissance began. It faced formidable difficulties. On their arrival in Israel, the two leaders found chaos. Those Jews who had remained had lost their identity. They had intermarried. The Sabbath was publicly desecrated. Religious laws had fallen into disuse.

The book of Nehemiah describes the event which was to prove the turning point. The people gathered in Jerusalem where Ezra, standing on a wooden platform, read to the assembled crowd from the Torah.

A group of Levites acted as instructors to the people, 'reading from the Book of the Law of God, making it clear and giving the meaning so that people could understand what was being read'. The population entered into a binding agreement to keep the Torah. The covenant, which had been in danger of being forgotten, was renewed. A new era of Jewish history began. From then on, for the next five centuries, though there were crises when significant segments of the population became acculturated and Hellenised, there was always a nucleus of Jews who remained loyal to Judaic principles.

Ezra represented a new kind of Jew, one who was to shape the character of the Jewish people from that time to this. Not a law-giver or a prophet, a king or a judge, neither a political nor a military leader, Ezra was the prototype of *the teacher as hero*. Under his influence, the ancient ideal of the people of the Torah became institutionalised. Public readings and explanations of the sacred texts became more widespread. By the second century BCE a system of community-funded schools had developed. Mass education, the first of its kind in the world, had begun.

The might-have-been is clear. The two tribes might have gone the way of the other ten. They too were conquered, sent into exile and exposed to the dangers of assimilation into a larger empire. But they resisted. They remained distinct, intact, a singular people. How was the might-have-been avoided? The lesson of the lost ten tribes had been learned. If the Jewish people was to survive, it needed to create a set of institutions through which its character could be sustained against the attritions of other cultures. It sought and found the structures of continuity. Judaism discovered a fundamental truth, one that has remained its unique characteristic among religious civilisations. *The best, indeed the only, defence of an identity is not military or political but educational.*

SURVIVING DESTRUCTION

In the first century CE a second crisis struck with devastating force. An ill-advised rebellion against Rome brought savage retaliation. The Roman forces led by Vespasian descended on the centres of Jewish resistance. In 70 CE Vespasian's son Titus brought the campaign to its climax with the siege of Jerusalem. The city was captured. The second Temple was destroyed. It was a fateful moment, though few of those who lived through it could have known for how long Jews would suffer its consequences. It was the beginning of the longest exile Israel had ever known. Not until the twentieth century would Jews again experience what it was like to be a sovereign people in their own land.

The disaster, completed sixty-five years later with the suppression of the Bar Kochba rebellion, was almost total. The bases of Jewish life lay in ruins. The Temple, symbol and centre of the nation, was gone. There were to be no more kings or prophets, serving priests or sacrifices within the foreseeable future. The loss of the first Temple had been accompanied by hope. There were prophets who foretold return and reconstruction. This time there were no such visions, at least none that carried immediate promise of fulfilment. The loss of the second Temple brought in its wake the danger of hopelessness.

Jewish tradition has rightly identified one moment as a symbol of the turning point. The Talmud relates how the sage Johanan ben Zakkai stood out against the Jews of his day. During the siege of Jerusalem, leaders within the city believed that they could prevail against Rome. Johanan knew that they were mistaken and argued unsuccessfully for surrender. Others believed that they would be saved by Divine intervention. The Messiah was about to come. Against them Johanan taught: 'If you have a sapling in your hand, and people say to you, "Behold, there is the Messiah" – go on with your planting and only then go out and receive him.' Johanan was a religious realist in an age of dangerous military and apocalyptic dreams.

Johanan, according to the Talmud, had himself smuggled out of Jerusalem and was taken to Vespasian. He made a simple request: 'Give me [the academy at] Yavneh and its sages.' Johanan predicated Jewish survival not on military victory or on the messianic age but on a house of study and a group of teachers.

Few decisions have had more lasting effects. For seventeen hundred years Jews became a people held together by study of Judaism's holy texts. In place of the Temple came the synagogue, the *yeshiva* and the *bet midrash*. In place of sacrifices came prayer, learning and the performance of good deeds. The mantle of leadership passed from kings, priests and prophets to the sage, the teacher who 'raised up many disciples'. Exiled, dispersed and deprived of power, a shattered nation was rebuilt through one instrumentality: education. Jews had lost their land, but they would not lose their identity. Physically scattered, they remained spiritually joined.

We are in an unusually good position to test Johanan ben Zakkai's strategy because his was not the only version of Jewish life. We know from Josephus and other sources that there were several Jewish tendencies in the late Second Commonwealth period. Johanan represented the group known as the Pharisees, who gave rise to the rabbis of the Mishnah and Talmud. There was a second and more powerful group known as the Sadducees, who were in general wealthier and more closely associated with the Temple and its priesthood. Josephus calls the third group the Essenes. They lived quasi-monastic lives in small separatist communities of which the Qumran sect, known to us through the Dead Sea Scrolls, may have been one.

For the Sadducees, the central dimension of Jewish life was the state and its institutions: the Sanhedrin and the Temple. For the Essenes it was the messianic age: they lived in imminent expectation of an apocalypse which would shake the foundations of the world. For the Pharisees, as we have seen, it was education. Their key institution was the school. Their figure of authority was the scholar. Their touchstone of Jewish identity was individual learning and observance of the Torah.

Neither Sadducees nor Essenes survived. Of their memory, only the most fragmentary traces remain. There was a time when both groups flourished and when each was convinced it held the key to the Jewish future. But history ruled otherwise. Once again, education proved the only route to continuity.

JEWISH CONTINUITY AFTER THE HOLOCAUST

The third crisis brings us to the present century and to what, in human terms, is the greatest tragedy ever to have struck the people of the covenant: the Holocaust. At the beginning of the twentieth century, four out of every five Jews lived in Europe. By the end of the Second World War the vast heartlands of European Jewry had been destroyed. The great powerhouses of rabbinic learning – Vilna, Volozhyn, Ponevetz, Mir – were gone. The citadels of the Jewish spirit had been reduced to ashes. Jewry's religious leaders and the communities from which they came had been murdered. At most, the survivors were 'a brand plucked from the burning'. Rarely has Judaism's everlasting light come closer to being extinguished.

What, spiritually, was left? Russian Jewry, the largest surviving Jewish community in Europe, lived under political and religious repression. America, though it was tolerant of Jews, had proved disastrous for Judaism. One wave of Jewish immigrants after another – first Spanish, then German, then East European – had acculturated, assimilated and disappeared. The new State of Israel, though it meant everything in physical and political terms, was aggressively secular. Ben Gurion had granted concessions to religious groups, but was confident that within a generation they would have disappeared.

What happened next will one day be told as one of the great acts of reconstruction in the religious history of mankind. A handful of Holocaust survivors and refugees set about rebuilding on new soil the world they had seen go up in flames. Rabbis Menahem Mendel Schneersohn, Aaron Kotler, Jacob Kamenetzky, Shragai Mendlowitz, Joseph Soloveitchik and others like them refused to yield to despair. While others responded to the Holocaust by building memorials, endowing lectureships, convening conferences and writing books, they built schools and communities and *yeshivot*. They urged their followers to marry and have children. They said: 'Our world has been shattered but not destroyed.' They said: 'Hitler brought death into the world, therefore let us bring life.' Within a generation Mir and Ponevetz, Lubavitch and Belz lived again, no longer in Europe, but in Israel and America.

Within a half-century, traditional Jewry has risen from the ashes to become the fastest growing and most influential force in Jewish life. It has achieved what all observers had hitherto thought impossible. It has shown that Torah can flourish in a secular Israel and an open America. It has proved that Jews in today's diaspora can experience demographic growth. It has brought about a revival in talmudic study that has no precedent since the great days of Babylonian Jewry. But it has done more. It has demonstrated in our time that the classic Jewish response to crisis remains the most powerful. Like Ezra, the *yeshivot* and Hasidic leaders concentrated on teaching. Like Johanan ben Zakkai they devoted themselves to raising up disciples.

Theirs, to repeat, was not the only response to the Holocaust. Other groups reacted differently. They built museums and monuments, funded chairs and periodicals, wrote Holocaust theology and sponsored visits to Auschwitz. A generation of young Jews, those who grew up in the 1970s and 1980s, has been liberally exposed to literature, films and lectures about the Holocaust, *and it is this generation which is choosing to marry out of Judaism at the rate of one in two*. The reason is not hard to find. As one Holocaust historian, disturbed by the obsessive interest in the Shoah, put it: our children will learn about the Greeks and how they lived, the Romans and how they lived, and the Jews and how they died. Unlike traditional Jewish education, Holocaust education *in itself* offers no meaning, no hope, no way of life. Unaccompanied by faith, it recapitulates the error of Lot's wife. The Holocaust is a black hole in human history, and if we stare at it too long we will turn to stone.

Jews never forgot the destruction of the first Temple, or the second. We mourn them on the Ninth of Av, and at every Jewish wedding we still break a glass in memory. It is 2,500 years since the first event and 1,900 since the second. So too, as long as Jews live, we will remember Auschwitz and Treblinka, Bergen-Belsen and Sobibor. But there is a Jewish way of remembering. For every tragedy, there is the promise of redemption. Every nightmare is succeeded by hope. We were never paralysed by our past, because we lived toward the future. That is why the Jewish response to catastrophe was to build schools and have children and create a Jewish future. The children of the *yeshiva* and Hasidic communities are their Holocaust memorials, made not of stone but of new life.

These three moments are seminal to an understanding of Jewish history. At each of them, the Jewish people confronted its own mortality. In none was the response that eventually proved successful by any means the obvious one. Who in his right mind would have suggested that the answer to the Babylonian conquest, the might of Rome or the devastation of the Holocaust lay in schools, teachers and houses of study? Yet Judaism's great visionaries, the architects of its survival, said just that.

Alternatives were tried. They failed. The ten tribes of the Northern kingdom disappeared. So did the Sadducees and Essenes. So, too, in our time are those diaspora communities that have failed to place Jewish education at the centre of their lives. In each case the survivors were ostensibly the weakest group. The southern kingdom of Judah was small in comparison to the kingdom of the north. The Pharisees were poorer and less powerful than the Sadducees. The Hasidic and *yeshiva* communities were, after the Shoah, a tattered remnant alongside the secular Jewries of America and Israel. In each case, however, the hypothesis of the sages was proved true. *So long as 'their mouths did not desist from study', the angel of death had no power over the Jewish people.* Those who set as their first priority the education of future generations were rewarded by Jewish continuity.

RECENT RESEARCH FINDINGS

Thus far the test of history. What of current research? Can we quantify the impact of Jewish education on Jewish identity? The answer is that we can.

The 1990 National Jewish Population Survey (NJPS) in the United States is, as we have noted, the most comprehensive study of a diaspora community undertaken in recent years. Its results are still being analysed. In March 1993 the first findings emerged of the effect of education on Jewish commitment, using the survey data. The study, by Sylvia Barack Fishman and Alice Goldstein, divided educational experience into four categories: (1) no Jewish education, (2) minimal education (less than three years of Jewish school or up to five of Sunday-only classes), (3) moderate education (three to five years of supplementary or day school, or six years of Sunday-only classes) and (4) substantial education (six or more years of supplementary or day school).

The findings were as follows: In the 25–44 year-old age group, those who had a substantial Jewish education are between six and ten times more likely to observe Jewish ritual than those whose Jewish education was minimal or non-existent. They are nearly three times more likely to belong to a Jewish organisation, three times more likely to be members of a synagogue and twenty per cent more likely to contribute to Jewish causes. They have more Jewish friends, are more opposed to intermarriage and are significantly less likely to marry out. *Of those with no Jewish education, only three out of ten are in-married. Of those with substantial Jewish education, the figure is eight out of ten.*

The authors conclude:

The 1990 NJPS data show us the strong correlation of Jewish education and enhanced Jewish identification. The mere fact of having received some Jewish education in childhood has little impact on Jewish attitudes and behaviours during the adult years. However, extensive Jewish education is definitively associated with higher measures of adult Jewish identification. Its impact is demonstrated in almost every area of public and private life.

Here then is further confirmation of the thesis that *the fate of the Jews in the diaspora was, is and predictably will be, determined by their commitment to education.* This proposition has been subjected to two tests, one against critical moments in Jewish history and the other against the most up-to-date research. Together, they demonstrate that Jewry's triumphs are triumphs of education. Our strategy for renewal is education. Our traditional strength, our greatest gift, our highest value is education.

Why then do we face a crisis of continuity? The sages said that when King David slipped, he momentarily stopped studying. In that instant his heart stopped beating. There is no more powerful metaphor for what has happened in the diaspora. For once, ancestral instinct has deserted us. We let education slip in our scale of priorities. Jews stopped studying. Three generations later, the Jewish heart is failing.

5
Priorities

The crisis in continuity has been sudden, devastating and unexpected. Intermarriage rates in America have risen almost ten times in twenty-five years. All the available evidence points to a similar erosion in Anglo-Jewry. The Jewish family, the crucible of Jewish continuity, is disintegrating before our eyes. This has happened in the space of one generation. Why?

The answer is complex. My concern in this book, however, is with one dimension only: our collective response and responsibility as a community. From this perspective, the answer is clear. It has happened *because for decades we have supported every Jewish cause except one: the Jewish future of our own children.*

Communally, we have given too little attention and too few resources to creating new generations of committed Jews. We have allocated too slender a share of our funds to Jewish education. Only belatedly have we recognised the need for Jewish schools. We have failed to recruit and train rabbis, educators and youth leaders. To those we have found, we have given too little reward, recognition and prestige. Jewish youth groups have limped for lack of funds. University chaplaincy has struggled to survive. Education has been the lowest of our priorities. We have lacked a strategy for Jewish continuity.

This has not been because we are uncharitable as a community. On the contrary, we have given voluntarily out of all proportion to our numbers. One of the most striking characteristics of the children of Israel was that, whenever they were asked, they gave. In the wilderness, when asked to contribute to the Golden Calf, they gave without demur. When asked to make a donation to the building of the Sanctuary they did likewise. The Golden Calf was an idol. The Sanctuary was the home of the Divine presence. There was nothing in common between them except this, that they both came into being through voluntary donations. The Talmud Yerushalmi expresses amazement: 'One cannot understand the nature of this people: if appealed to for the Calf they give; if appealed to for the Sanctuary they give.' Jewishly, to live was to give. It still is.

However, what has attracted our philanthropy for the past thirty years has been other places and other times. Our minds have been dominated by the Shoah and the State of Israel. We have monitored antisemitism and funded Holocaust studies. We have scanned the horizons of Central and Eastern Europe for danger signals of resurgent hatred. We have lived vicariously in Israel's pain and glory. We have helped Israel build universities and engage in urban renewal. We have watched the miraculous rescue of Ethiopian Jewry. We have campaigned for and finally witnessed the liberation and exodus of the Jews of Russia. These were urgent, important, necessary endeavours. But in the meantime we neglected our own future: our children. The Holocaust, Israel, Russia, Ethiopia, are sometime or somewhere else. But to be able to remember the past we must also have a future. To be of lasting help to others, we must first ensure our own survival.

Why then has the crisis of continuity happened? It is because as a community, and without intending to, we have let it happen. The evidence is presented below. But first I want to consider two principles of Jewish law. They tell us much about how Jews lived and what they valued. They tell us more about how they succeeded in raising new generations of Jews. They tell us, in short, what our priorities should be today.

A MEETING

Twenty-five years ago I had an encounter which has stayed in my mind ever since. The year was 1968. I was then a philosophy student at Cambridge University. It was not an environment conducive to religious belief. Scepticism or atheism were the order of the day. But the Six Day War had awakened my interest in Jewish identity, and I decided to travel to America, the home of Jewry's leading philosophers and thinkers, to find out for myself whether a cogent case could be made for Jewish faith in the modern age. It was there that I met a famous Hasidic Rebbe and heard for the first time a great principle of Jewish law.

Ushered in to the Rebbe's study, I bombarded him with a series of questions about Judaism. His answers were courteous, brief, to the point and unemotional. It was a stylised encounter, a debate rather than a meeting of minds. My questions were predictable, the Rebbe's answers conventional. Then suddenly the atmosphere changed. I suggested that the Rebbe's kind of faith was too parochial. It was concerned only with Judaism and Jews. Surely there was a world outside with which we, as Jews, had to be engaged. There was a global over-population. There was famine in Africa. There were political conflicts which had nothing to do with Jews, but in which we were none the less implicated as citizens of the world.

The Rebbe smiled, leaned forward and looked up for the first time. Staring straight into my eyes, he said: '*Aniyei ircha kodmim*, the poor of your own town take precedence. You are right', he continued. 'We have many duties. But there are priorities among them. According to Jewish law, our first priority is to ensure the well-being of those closest to us. We cannot save the world without first saving ourselves.'

The Rebbe was quoting from talmudic tractate of *Baba Metzia* which states that if there is a choice between assisting the members of your family and helping citizens of your town, your family takes precedence. If the choice is between your town and another city, your town takes precedence. The principle is echoed in many other places in Jewish law.

The ultimate aim of charity, according to *halakhah* is to promote neither generosity on the part of the giver nor gratitude on the part of the recipient, important though these principles are. It is *to create independence*. So we find, according to Maimonides, that the highest form of *tzedakah* is 'that of the person who assists a poor Jew by providing him with a gift or a loan or by accepting him into a business partnership or by helping him find employment – in a word, by putting him where he can dispense with other people's aid.'

So an individual or a town may not impoverish themselves by giving their possessions away, for this solves one problem at the cost of creating another. An individual or a community must first ensure that they are self-sufficient. They are then in a position to help others, now and in the long run.

It is this idea that lies behind Hillel's famous aphorism: 'If I am not for myself, who will be? But if I am only for myself, what am I?' We believe in collective responsibility, in giving to others. *Tzedakah* is a cardinal Jewish virtue. But first we believe in personal responsibility, in creating our own independence and viability. And what applies to individuals also applies to communities. *Domestic causes take priority over others*. Not *exclusive* priority, for we must help other communities in need. But priority none the less. For if we fail to secure our own viability as a Jewish community we will eventually be in no position to help others, and the roles will be reversed. Instead of giving assistance, we will need to receive it.

A QUESTION OF PRECEDENCE

That is the first axiom. The second was brought home to me in a most curious way. About a year ago I received an invitation to lunch with the Prime Minister at Chequers. At the same time I received an invitation to take part in the opening ceremony of a new Jewish school in London. Both events were on the same day, at roughly the same time. I could not attend both. Which took precedence?

A famous Mishnah states:

> Rabbi Hanina, the deputy High Priest, said: Pray for the welfare of the government, since were it not that they feared it, people would swallow one another alive.

Since the days of the prophet Jeremiah, we have 'sought the welfare of the city' in which we live. We value the rule of law, the duties of citizenship, and maintaining good relationships with our neighbours and with the government. But there is another rabbinic teaching in Maimonides' law code, the *Mishneh Torah*, which states:

> If a town has made no provision for the Jewish education of its children, then its inhabitants are to be excommunicated until teachers have been appointed ... for the world only exists in virtue of the sound of children at their studies.

Nothing could more vividly illustrate Judaism's scale of priorities. *Governments sustain society, but education sustains the world.* On that occasion I regretfully declined the Prime Minister's invitation and opened the school.

Consistently throughout our history, we have placed education at the very top of our priorities, not just in theory but in practice, and not only as individuals but as a community. In his *Outline of History*, H.G. Wells noted that 'the Jewish religion, because it was a literature-sustained religion, led to the first efforts to provide elementary education for all children in the community'.

Nearly two thousand years before Europe, Jews had created a system of universal, free, compulsory education. Tuition for teenagers was begun by Shimon ben Shetach in the first century BCE. Before the destruction of the second Temple, Joshua ben Gamla had established a comprehensive network of primary schools throughout Judea. Towards the end of the first century CE, Josephus could write that 'should any one of our nation be asked about our laws, he will repeat them as readily as his own name. The result of our thorough education in our laws from the very dawn of intelligence is that they are, as it were, engraved on our souls.'

By the fourth century CE educational policy had become so thorough that Rava was able to introduce a rule limiting the maximum class size to 25 (or 40 if there was both a teacher and an assistant), the first such regulation in history. Higher and adult education – in the form of the *yeshiva* and *bet midrash* – are even older Jewish traditions, and it would be difficult to find a counterpart, even today, to the Jewish ideal of life-long learning.

Sustaining such an infrastructure was costly, and as a matter of principle, the burden of funding was placed not only on parents but also on the community as a whole. In fifteenth-century Spain, for example, the Jewish community established a series of ordinances to ensure that every child received a Jewish education. The revenue was obtained from taxes on meat and wine, circumcisions, weddings and funerals. The Valladolid synod of 1432 ordered 'that every community of fifteen householders (or more) shall be obliged to maintain a qualified elementary teacher to instruct their children in Scripture .. The parents shall be obliged to send their children to that teacher, and each shall pay him in accordance with their means. If this revenue should prove inadequate, the community shall be obliged to supplement it.' Every community of forty or more households was instructed to provide advanced as well as elementary schooling. The Chief Rabbi of Castile was authorised to divert money from wealthier to impoverished communities to subsidise struggling schools.

Similar, if less detailed, provisions existed elsewhere in Europe. The fees of poorer children, and sometimes the salaries of teachers, were paid by the community. The funds were raised by taxes, or obligatory contributions on being called to the Torah, or house-to-house collections. In twelfth-century France, Rabbenu Tam ruled that when there was a shortage of funds for education, money designated for other purposes could be diverted to schools and teachers. The quality of education varied from country to country and from century to century, but there was one common factor. Until the modern era there was virtually no European Jewish community, however small, without a school and teachers. Benjamin of Tudela, travelling in Provence in 1165, could report that in Posquières, a town of some forty Jews, there was a great *yeshiva*. Marseilles, whose Jewish population was three hundred, was 'a city of *geonim* [outstanding scholars] and sages.'

Documents have recently been published which shed vivid light on Jewish communal priorities. They come from Moravia (today's Czech Republic) in the late seventeenth and early eighteenth centuries. Jews in Central Europe had been devastated by the Thirty Years' War, 1618–1648, and by the Chmielnicki massacres in Poland, 1648–9. Community life came to a standstill. As normal conditions slowly returned, Jews began to rebuild their institutions. The documents date from that period and are the *takanot* or ordinances of various Jewish communities. They relate to the districts of Gaya (1650), Brody (1677), Kremsier (1681 and 1694), Goeding (1689) and Butschowitz (1707). Each of them is concerned with one thing: rebuilding *yeshivot*, academies of Jewish study. Every community was exhorted to establish a house of study and finance both it and its students, or incur fines.

The *takanah* of Kanitz (1713), having laid down provisions for the use of communal funds to establish five *yeshivot*, continues:

We have been taught by our ancient rabbis to be especially concerned with poor students, because it is from the poor students that the Torah will flow. Now, there are communities where the poor cannot support a teacher from their funds, while there are rich Jews who refuse to contribute to the support of teachers because they claim that they have no sons of their own, or they use some other excuse. In such cases the community council must hire teachers so that the students learn, each one according to his capacity, and help those parents who have sons, so that not one of them is without Torah learning. Each father, too, must learn with his son ...

The first thing these devastated townships were concerned to do, once peace returned, was to reconstruct their educational system. In the words of one of the documents: 'Unless there are calves, there will be no oxen.' Without Jewishly educated children, there will be no Jewish future. There can be no more eloquent testimony to Jewish priorities than these records of communities piecing themselves together after catastrophe. While Europe built armies, Jews built schools.

So if the first principle of community is that domestic causes take priority, the second is that among these causes, education takes precedence. The logic of the second principle is the same as the first. Before anything else, a community must establish its viability, which means its continuity. It must secure the Jewish future of its children, which means their education. If these preconditions are satisfied, all else will follow. If they are lacking, all else will fail. Such are the teachings of Jewish law on communal priorities.

ANGLO-JEWISH GIVING

In the light of these axioms, what are we to make of the following figures, published by the Charities Aid Foundation in *Charity Trends 1992*? They represent the amounts given to Jewish causes in 1991.

Charity	Total Voluntary Income £000
Jewish Philanthropic Association	24,662
Society of Friends of Jewish Refugees	4,800
Jewish National Fund	3,535
Friends of the Hebrew University	2,232
Jerusalem Foundation	1,172
British Technion Society	1,096
Society of Friends of Federation of Women Zionists	1,048
CBF World Jewish Relief	2,019
Jewish Care	6,914
Nightingale House	2,371
Ravenswood Foundation	2,221
Norwood Child Care	1,218
Jewish Educational Development Trust	945
Friends of Zionist Federation Educational Trust	740

These figures tell us a number of things about Anglo-Jewry. First, they indicate that we are an exceptionally generous community. The Jewish tradition of *tzedakah* is alive and well. Second, they signal that Israel is at the heart of our lives. This too is an age-old Jewish tradition. For centuries when we prayed, we prayed towards Jerusalem. When we celebrated, we paused to remember Zion. Today when we give, we give to Israel. Third, the needs of welfare continue to move us to compassion. *Gemillat hasadim* (practical kindness), said the sages, is one of the three pillars on which the world stands. Jewishly, it still is. These are all achievements of which we should be proud. There are few if any other religious or ethnic groups who regularly show such generosity and collective practical concern.

However, the chart reveals a fourth fact, namely that Jewish education, the core of continuity, is the lowest of all our communal priorities. Dramatically so. In a year in which nearly £40 million was raised for Israel and £13 million for welfare, the two major educational fund-raising bodies, JEDT and ZFET, managed to elicit less than

£1.7 million between them. Judged by this measure *we allocated to education one-eighth of what we gave to welfare and less than one-twentieth of what we gave to Israel.* Or, to put it differently, *we gave more to one university in Israel than to the leading educational charities in Anglo-Jewry combined.* This is not in accordance with Jewish tradition nor is it a fact in which we can take pride.

To be sure, 1991 was an exceptional year for fund-raising for Israel. It was a bad year for education. And the Charities Aid Foundation lists only the major charities, omitting smaller amounts raised for individual Jewish schools. Recently, however, the Board of Deputies released information about *all* Jewish charities in 1990. This showed that of the £47 million raised that year, 53.1 per cent went to Israel, 35.2 per cent to welfare and 10.1 per cent to education and youth. This figure is hardly more encouraging. For it shows that even in a good year, the entire educational budget of Anglo-Jewry – capital and running costs, central and local charities, schools and youth groups – amounts to less than a third of what we spend on welfare and a fifth of what we send to Israel.

If 1990 was bad for Jewish education, 1991 was worse. The 1992 figures are not yet available, but in absolute terms they are bound to be worse still. As the impact of the recession on Anglo-Jewry has deepened, one Jewish educational body after another has faced financial crisis. A secondary school in North East London closed. A primary school in North West London warned parents that the same fate might be in store for it in a year's time. The Association of Jewish Sixth Formers came to the brink of closure. The two largest providers of Jewish Day Schools, the United Synagogue and the Zionist Federation Educational Trust, both found themselves in financial difficulties. The United Synagogue's Adult Education department was terminated. So was its provision of Jewish instruction at non-Jewish schools. The recession has had a devastating effect on all Jewish communal institutions, sustained as they are by voluntary contributions. But the first and worst casualty has been education.

Admittedly, these figures do not take into account what private individuals spend on Jewish tuition for their children. They refer only to charitable donations, to what we give to others and to the common good. My sole concern in this book, however, is our fate *as a community*. Traditionally, and according to Jewish law, education is not just a private duty. It is a collective, communal responsibility. Individuals can arrange tuition for their children. But they cannot build schools, devise curricula, recruit and train teachers, make provisions for smaller and less affluent communities and create a living Jewish environment outside the home. These things can only be done by the community as a whole, and by each of us contributing our share. That is what we are not doing, and that is why we are losing our children.

Patterns of giving reflect our scale of values. Communally, in Anglo-Jewry, we have broken the two fundamental rules of Jewish giving. We have not heeded the principle of *aniyei ircha kodmin*, that domestic causes take precedence over others. Nor have we followed the rule that, more than any other, has distinguished us from other peoples and faiths. We have not put education first.

GOOD NEWS, BAD NEWS

We should not exaggerate the bad news. Good things have happened in Anglo-Jewry in the past twenty-five years. In 1971, the then Chief Rabbi, Lord Jakobovits, launched the Jewish Educational Development Trust which raised the profile of Jewish education, built two schools and raised funds for a variety of educational projects, including some in the field of teacher-training. More recently, the United Synagogue has significantly enlarged its educational remit, culminating in the recent opening of two new schools, the Hillel Primary School in Southgate (1992) and the King Solomon High School in Redbridge (1993). In the past ten years adult education has flourished, and there has recently been great interest in the concept of family education.

The bad news should not be exaggerated, but it should not be under-estimated either. We have raised capital sums to build schools, but not the funds to keep them going. We have concentrated on buildings rather than people (what the Americans call the Jewish 'edifice complex'). We have focused, rightly, on day schools while, wrongly, neglecting the many other aspects of a continuity-creating environment such as youth groups and informal, adult and family education. More of our children receive intensive Jewish day school education than a generation ago, but many others are receiving little or no tuition at all. The JED'I' Think Tank Report (*Securing Our Future*, 1992) showed that beyond the age of thirteen only half of our children continue in any form of Jewish instruction. By the age of sixteen this has dropped to one in six, and by the age of seventeen, to one in ten. It is this group – the half whose Jewish education is slight and growing ever less – who are most liable to leave the community through intermarriage or disaffiliation. Meanwhile, the recession has put even existing facilities at risk.

Anglo-Jewry lacks an overall strategy for education, for continuity and for communal priorities as a whole. As a result, in common with America, we have done what no Jewish community did between the destruction of the second Temple and the nineteenth century. We have neglected our intellectual, spiritual and cultural environment and the concept of a 'learning society'. Worst of all for a people that has always cared for its future, we have put the Jewish needs of our children last.

It is not that we are ungenerous to Jewish causes. On the contrary, as the figures show, we have given liberally to Israel, Jewish welfare and many other aspects of community life. Nor are we, as parents, ungenerous to our children. If anything we have been over-indulgent parents. Certainly, when it comes to our children's secular education we want the best and are prepared to pay for it. So we are willing to give to Jewish causes and we are willing to give to our children. What we seem unwilling to do is to give to a Jewish cause when the Jewish cause *is* our children.

THE MESSAGE FROM ISRAEL

This is worse than untraditional. It is little less than suicidal. Whatever our commitments as Jews, they can only be sustained in the long run if there is going to be a next generation of Jews. If we care about Israel, how will this help us or Israel if our grandchildren no longer feel any ties with the Jewish people and its homeland? If we care about welfare, how will this help those in need fifty years from now, if our grandchildren are no longer part of a community that recognises the need for collective responsibility and care?

Whatever we value, we wish to see continued by our children and theirs. If we care about anything beyond ourselves, we do not wish to see it come to an end with ourselves and our generation. Our present patterns of Jewish giving, if continued into the future, are destined to end in the collapse of Jewish life in the diaspora for all but a minority of the most intensely religious. We will have given to Israel but not to our own community's future. We will have given to the old but not the young. We will have given to Jewish defence against external enemies but not to Jewish defence against the most powerful enemy of all: internal Jewish ignorance and indifference.

Unprecedentedly, this message is now coming not only from religious leaders but from secular figures as well, and not only in the diaspora but even in Israel itself. In the past, Israel has been candid in its demands of the diaspora. It has called for support for Israel: political, financial and above all by way of *aliyah*. Never before have Israeli politicians called on Jewish communities abroad to start supporting *themselves* through Jewish education.

However, in the Knesset on 22 December 1992 Labour member Eli Dayan called on Israel to energise the diaspora to save itself from assimilation. He pleaded for a concerted Jewish effort to mobilise resources in a worldwide Jewish educational campaign. President Chaim Herzog expressed a similar sentiment in a letter to me in October 1992:

> For many years I have insisted, at every conceivable opportunity, both privately and in public appearances, that Jewish education in the diaspora is paramount and must be accorded a very high priority in the activities of every Jewish community. *This is not only in the interests of the communities abroad. It is also of vital interest to the State of Israel.* Israel's centrality in the Jewish world assumes the existence of a strong and vibrant Jewish community abroad and Jewish education in the diaspora is, therefore, of the greatest possible importance.

The inescapable logic is that Israel will still need the support of the diaspora in the future. The Jewish State needs there to *be* a diaspora in the future. If Jews assimilate, Israel is the loser. It loses friends. It loses funds. It loses potential *olim*. Until recently the needs of Israel were immediate. There were wars to fight, Jewries to be rescued, immigrants to be absorbed. But with the rescue of Russian and Ethopian Jewry and the beginnings of a peace process, Israel has had a chance to draw breath and think long-term. Its most farsighted politicians have now realised that the diaspora, in its dedication to Israel, has neglected itself and that this poses a threat to the Jewish future as a whole.

THE FOURTH GENERATION

The problems of Jewish continuity have arisen because we have broken the two great rules of Jewish giving. We have given to Israel at the expense of our own viability. And we have been generous to the old at the expense of the young. Israel and welfare need our undiminished support. But so *and in equal measure* does education. Had we acted on this earlier we would have saved ourselves and our children much grief. Why then did we not do so?

For several generations, indeed for more than a century, Jewish education was not at the forefront of our concerns for reasons which will be examined in the next chapter. Nevertheless, nothing devastating happened as a result. Jews continued to identify as Jews. They joined synagogues. They married other Jews. They had Jewish children and raised them as Jews. Jewish life continued on the basis of habit, memory and tradition regardless of the fact that little was being done to renew it by Jewish study. If it could continue in this way for a century, why not longer, even indefinitely? We have only belatedly discovered that this is an illusion. What has changed? Why is this generation different from all other generations? The answer lies in what I call *the fourth-generation phenomenon*.

My grandparents were not born in this country. Many, even most, of the Jews in Britain had grandparents who came here in the great wave of immigration from Eastern Europe between 1880 and 1914. We are Anglo-Jews of the third generation.

It is an almost universal law that inherited wealth lasts three generations, not more. The same applies to inherited Judaism. Ours is the last generation that can still remember *booba* and *zeida* from the *heim*, with their fluent Yiddish and undiminished *Yiddishkeit*. *Ours is the last generation for whom Jewish identity can be sustained by memory alone.*

The Rebbe of Ger once pointed out that the 'four sons' of the *Haggadah* represent four generations. The wise son is the immigrant generation who still lives the traditions of the 'home'. The rebellious son is the second generation, forsaking Judaism for social integration. The 'simple' son is the third generation, confused by the mixed messages of religious grandparents and irreligious parents. But the child who cannot even ask the question is the fourth generation. For the child of the fourth generation no longer has memories of Jewish life in its full intensity.

Our children are children of the fourth generation. Already, it is clear that what we took for granted, they do not. They do not take it for granted that they will belong to an Orthodox synagogue or indeed any synagogue. They do not take it for granted that they will marry, or marry another Jew, or stay married. They do not take it for granted that they will have Jewish children or that it is important to do so. *Nothing* can be taken for granted in the fourth generation, least of all in a secular, open society in which even a common moral code is lacking.

The 'fourth-generation phenomenon' explains what is otherwise inexplicable, namely that the crisis of Jewish continuity has occurred in a single generation. To repeat the statistic at the heart of our concern: the intermarriage rate among young Jews in the United States has risen from six per cent in 1960 to 57 per cent in 1985. The rise in mixed marriage, non-marriage and divorce, and the corresponding fall in religious observance and Jewish affiliation, have occurred suddenly and with astonishing speed. There is no obvious explanation. There have been no dramatic shifts in the diaspora in respect of tolerance on the one hand, antisemitism on the other. The environment in which Jews live has not significantly changed. Why then have Jews changed? The answer is that the Jews who have chosen not to remain Jews are the great-grandchildren of those who arrived in Britain and America to escape the pogroms of Eastern Europe in the 1880s. They are the Jews of the fourth generation.

In the absence of a determined effort to transmit our traditions to our children, Jewish identity persists for three generations, not longer. The fact that the erosion is gradual rather than sudden allows us to remain blind to the process for many decades. We can do so no more. We live with the symptoms, to the point where for most of us it has become an entirely open question as to whether we will have Jewish grandchildren. The trend can be reversed, but only by a clear re-instatement of classical Jewish priorities. If we are to have a future as a Jewish community we can no longer let our children be the last and least of our concerns, as we have done until now.

There is a wise aphorism which states: *When all else fails, read the instructions.* That surely applies in the case of Anglo-Jewry. Jewish law provides clear guidance as to how to allocate our charitable funds: to domestic causes first, and to education above all else. We have ignored those rules for several generations and it has cost us dearly. But mere exhortation is unlikely to make us change habits which have become so deeply ingrained.

We have now reached the heart of the argument. I have spoken about the miracle of Jewish continuity, stretching as it does across three-quarters of the history of human civilisation. I have documented the crisis we have reached in our time. I have argued that Jewish identity in the past was sustained through education, and I submitted that hypothesis to the test of history and recent research. In this chapter, I have shown how this hypothesis holds good in the present. We face a crisis of continuity because we have failed to invest in education.

An obvious question now arises. How, if education is the key to the perpetuation of Jewish identity, did we ever come to neglect it? If the solution to the problem of continuity is so clearly signalled by every lesson of Jewish history and every instinct of the Jewish imagination, how then did we miss it? How did we fail to read the instructions? Unless we find the answer to this question, we will not fully grasp what has changed in the terms and circumstances of Jewish life. We will fail to comprehend the most important thesis of this book: that we are entering a new era in modern Jewish history.

6
From Integration to Survival to Continuity

A sense of history is part of what it is to be a Jew. Admittedly, much of Judaism is timeless – our beliefs, our values, our way of life. One of our most potent symbols is the *ner tamid*, the everlasting light that, like the bush Moses saw in the desert, 'burns and is not consumed'. We are an eternal people bound to the eternal God. The days, the years, the centuries pass, but Judaism and the Jewish people remain.

But there is another dimension to Jewish life: an acute sensitivity to time. Jews were the first people to see 'the hand of God' in history. In one of the classics of modern Jewish scholarship, *Zakhor*, Yosef Hayim Yerushalmi writes:

It was ancient Israel that first assigned a decisive significance to history and thus forged a new world-view . . . 'The heavens', in the words of the psalmist, might still 'declare the glory of the Lord', but it was human history that revealed His will and purpose . . . Far from attempting a flight from history, biblical religion allows itself to be saturated by it and is inconceivable apart from it.

This sense of time yielded an entirely new type of religious personality, the *prophet*. Unlike Moses who transmitted laws which were 'everlasting statutes', the other prophets spoke to their own generation and its challenges. For some, such as Jeremiah, the challenge was exile. For others, like Ezekiel, it was preparation for return. 'Each generation', said the sages, 'produces its own search and its own leaders.'

There are several Jewish commandments to *count time*. There is the counting of the Omer, the forty-nine days between Pesach and Shavuot. There is the institution of the Jubilee, with its command to count forty-nine years and declare the fiftieth holy. Through these disciplines, we learn that each day and year contains its unique challenges and opportunities: 'Teach us to number our days that we may get a heart of wisdom.' And there is yet another, if less precise, mandate which might be called the prophetic imperative. This tells us to count *epochs*. The prophetic challenge is to identify an age and its problems. Indeed, the inner history of Israel could be written solely in terms of what each era saw as its particular challenge and opportunity.

My thesis is this: we are entering a new era in modern Jewish life, one which presents quite different problems from those which have dominated the Jewish agenda hitherto. The crisis of continuity has arisen *now* because we are still using the priorities and strategies of an earlier age. The problem is not that it is difficult to create continuity. It is that for many years past, continuity has not been our dominant concern. There were other urgent issues which demanded our attention. The situation has now changed, but we have not yet responded by redirecting our efforts. The result is that we find ourselves fighting yesterday's battles instead of today's.

INTEGRATION

What were yesterday's battles? They can be summarised in two words: *integration* and *survival*.

From the nineteenth century until 1967 the key word of European and American Jewish life was *integration*. The secularisation of the West and the rise of the nation state offered Jews the possibility of becoming full participants in the majority society and its culture, something that had been impossible since the age of Constantine in the third century. Emancipation bestowed on Jews the full range of civic rights. But it carried a price, namely that Jews passed through what John Murray Cuddihy has called the 'ordeal of civility' and adapted to the manners and mores of Europe. It meant the end of a certain kind of Jewish apartness and the beginning of a journey 'out of the ghetto'.

Most Jews welcomed the new age, but it quickly proved to be the start of a prolonged crisis of identity which has haunted western Jewry to this day. For some Jews the inner conflict between being an heir to the covenant at Sinai and a citizen of the modern state was simply too great. Some assimilated out of Judaism altogether. Others adapted its demands until, instead of being the way of life of a particular people, Judaism became the 'religion of ethical universalism'. At the other extreme, there were those who rejected modern culture and decided that if Jews were to remain Jews, they would have to choose not integration but segregation.

In Britain, however, Jews found a society that was both more tolerant and less ideologically driven than elsewhere in Europe. Most found themselves able to reconcile their twin identities. The traditionalism of English life harmonised with the traditionalism of Jewish sentiment and produced, by and large, a happy marriage. Nineteenth-century Anglo-Jews could point to such role-models as Sir Moses Montefiore who could move with equal ease between the City and the royal court, and the synagogue and the *bet midrash*. In Chief Rabbi Nathan Marcus Adler they had a religious leader who combined unbending Orthodoxy with Victorian decorum. Even Benjamin Disraeli, who had been converted to Christianity as a child, could refer to his Jewish origins with pride. All this was in marked contrast to the tormented inner struggles of Central and Eastern European Jewry and the reckless abandonment of tradition by the Jews of the United States.

The pursuit of integration had a marked effect on Jewish education. Victorian England had Jewish schools. But their primary purpose was to protect Jewish children from the then active efforts of Christian missionaries. Beyond this, as Israel Finestein puts it, Jewish schools were seen as 'valuable instruments for anglicisation'. They were set up largely to assist the Jewish working class – above all, the new immigrants – to become vocationally trained and to adjust to English society. In a sermon delivered at the New West End Synagogue in 1887, Hermann Adler, Nathan's son and successor as Chief Rabbi, spelled out the prevailing philosophy of the Jewish establishment of his day. Their task, he declared, was 'to anglicise, humanise and civilise' the new East European immigrants, and 'to enable them to become absorbed in the intelligent, industrious, independent wage-earning classes of the country'.

Within its own terms, this policy worked remarkably well. The story of successive generations of Anglo-Jewish immigrants has been one of rapid rise 'out of the ghetto' and, in many cases, to public prominence in the arts and sciences, business and industry, academic and political life. Jews acculturated with astonishing speed and became the very models of upward mobility. By and large, too, the innate conservatism and tolerance of British society worked to the benefit of Jewish identity. There were moments of awkwardness and occasional outbreaks of antisemitism. For the most part, however, Jews were content to remain Jews and join and occasionally attend synagogues. Integration was possible, and few other Jewries achieved it with so little drama and apparently so painlessly.

SURVIVAL

The turning point, in world Jewish terms, came in 1967. Looking back at that moment some eighteen years later, two American scholars, Steven Cohen and Leonard Fein, described it as the time when the dominant theme of diaspora Jewish life turned 'from integration to survival'.

The catalyst for this change was Israel, specifically the threat to its existence in the weeks leading up to the Six Day War. The effect of the 1967 war was felt no less in American Jewry. It was one of those rare moments – like the Warsaw Ghetto uprising – which can fairly be said to have changed Jewish consciousness and left its permanent mark on our collective personality. Ironically, it was in 1967 that diaspora Jewry finally discovered the Holocaust, which had taken place more than twenty years before. It took the threat of a second devastation to unlock the floodgates of feeling about the first.

There is a difference between history and memory, especially group memory: between what happened and the way we frame our perceptions of what happened. Israel's battle for survival in 1967 came to be seen by a whole generation of American Jews as something more than a remarkable military victory, and as something other than a miracle in the traditional sense. It became a symbol, an emblem of a new Jewish identity. Jews had been sentenced to death in the *Shoah*. Israel now came face to face with the spectre of a second holocaust at the hands of its hostile neighbours. But the Jewish people survived. Indeed, that was our fate. Jews are the people who are threatened but who survive.

The new survivalism was significantly different in mood and attitude from the old integrationism. Israel became far more prominent in Jewish life worldwide. Several commentators were moved to say that Israel had become the religion of the diaspora. Activism began to permeate Jewry. Jews were to be found less often praying to God than raising funds, mobilising support and engaged in political lobbying on behalf of Israel or Soviet Jewry or the fight against antisemitism.

The ideal of integration had been based on a fundamentally optimistic view of human nature. This was best expressed in the Pittsburgh Platform of 1885, a statement of the then prevailing views of American Reform: 'We recognise in the modern era of universal culture of heart and intellect the approach of Israel's great Messianic hope for the establishment of the kingdom of truth, justice and peace among all men.' Reason and tolerance would prevail. Prejudice would die. Less than a century later, those hopes were finally dashed. Accordingly, survivalism took a darker view. The Holocaust had revealed man's persisting capacity for evil in the midst of great civilisation. Israel's continuing isolation showed the sheer tenacity of antisemitism, now transmuted into anti-Zionism. For Jews, the modern world had proved to be a dangerous place indeed.

This gave impetus to a new Jewish particularism. Jews found themselves suddenly interested not in what made them the same as everyone else but in what made them different. A generation of young Jews began to search for their roots and lost religious heritage. They took the 'path of return'. Across a wide spectrum of religious affiliation, Jews developed a new interest in ritual – the codes and actions of Jewish difference. They became far readier than any previous generation since emancipation to give public expression to their Jewishness. Israel had given them pride. Thoughts of the Holocaust had given them defiance.

There was one other factor in this transformation. It had nothing to do with Israel or indeed with Jewishness as such. The 1960s were also the time when a certain cultural model began to be challenged and overthrown: what became known in America as the 'melting pot' and in Britain as assimilation. This was the idea that a society possessed a single dominant culture into which all minorities must eventually merge. Instead, a new model emerged – pluralism or multiculturalism – which held that society was a mosaic of different groups with differing ways of life, none of which held primacy over any other. This change, along with the epic events in Israel, profoundly affected Jews.

To understand why, we must remember the deep effects of secularisation on the Jewish community, most notably in America. In the 1960s, Gerhard Lenski found Jews to be markedly less 'religious' in their attitudes than either Protestants or Catholics, a finding which remained true in the mid-1980s. Clearly, this signalled a crisis for any traditional Jewish identity. To be Jewish, whether in the ancient or the modern world, was to be a member of a people defined by its faith and religious code. But the constellation of forces in the 1960s now made possible a quite different definition. The struggles of the Holocaust and the State of Israel could be seen as less to do with God than with the Jewish people and their will to survive. The pluralism of contemporary American life gave Jews a mandate to continue to survive. Jews could now see themselves as something other than a *religious community.* They were, and increasingly saw themselves as, an *ethnic group*.

These changes took place most dramatically in America. Nevertheless, they had an effect on Anglo-Jewry as well. Here too, the *Shoah* and Israel become touchstones of Jewish identity. Fund-raising and political activism took on a new significance in Jewish life. At any time before 1967 there could be no doubt as to which were the most significant positions of lay leadership within the community. They were the President of the Board of Deputies and the President of the United Synagogue, the two positions which externally and internally epitomised Anglo-Jewry as a religious community. Today, Anglo-Jewish leaders are as likely to be drawn to the secular fields of Israel, welfare and defence as to the synagogue and representation.

Britain is a less plausible home than America for the idea that Jews are simply an ethnic group. There are fewer Jews here, too few to sustain a viable ethnic subculture. Besides, pluralism and the associated separation of religion and state never belonged to British values as they did to America, the land of immigrants. None the less, significant numbers of young Jews do now see their identity in essentially ethnic terms. For them, Jewish belonging is a matter of mixing with other Jews, supporting Israel and fighting antisemitism and has no especially religious connotation.

THE PASSING OF AN ERA

Just as integrationism apparently resolved the 'problem' of being Jewish in a modern secular society, so survivalism rallied Jewish energies at a time of flagging commitment. It highlighted the role which the State of Israel played in making Jews worldwide feel more secure and more capable of action when particular diaspora communities are under threat of persecution. Survivalism played no small part in the worldwide Jewish response to the plight of Soviet and Ethiopian Jewry. Equally importantly, it gave Jews a way of seeing themselves as part of a single people at a time when religious and cultural differences had penetrated so deeply that perhaps nothing else was capable of uniting them. Not all Jews could relate to the concept of the covenant at Sinai. Most, however, could identify with the idea that, but for an accident of history, they might have been victims of Hitler's Final Solution.

The idea of survival energised Jews for a generation. But it can do so no longer. The turning point has been the realisation, in the 1990s, that young diaspora Jews are disaffiliating at an unprecedented rate. *Jewish commitment to survival has not proved strong enough to ensure that Jews survive.*

It took some time before the extent of the crisis was understood. As we noted in Chapter 2, in the mid-1980s a school of American Jewish sociologists, known as transformationists, argued that the Jewish community was *not* endangered by high rates of intermarriage. If the non-Jewish partner converted, or if at least half the children of mixed marriages were raised as Jews, there would be no net loss to the community and perhaps even a gain. Such was the argument of figures like Charles Silberman and Calvin Goldscheider.

That optimism has now proved dramatically unfounded. Few non-Jewish partners in mixed marriages convert, and few bring up their children as Jews. This is so, despite the fact that the liberal denominations in America have virtually abandoned preconditions for conversion, and have chosen, through the controversial 'patrilineal' ruling of 1983, to recognise the children of Jewish fathers and non-Jewish mothers as Jews. In short, despite every liberal accommodation to mixed marriage, the American Jewish community is losing Jews at a prodigious rate.

Anglo-Jewry is different from American Jewry. On the whole, we are more traditional, more affiliated and better educated Jewishly. Nor have the issues been debated here with the same clarity and vigour as across the Atlantic. None the less, the experience of American Jewry in the 1990s allows us to see the deep shortcomings of survivalism as a philosophy of Jewish life. Paradoxically, survivalism fails as a strategy for survival.

It makes sense when what is at stake is *physical* survival. When lives are at risk or freedoms are in danger we need no further justification for our concern. Physical survival has dominated twentieth-century Jewish history. The Holocaust and the State of Israel have been central to our thoughts. The Holocaust stands as the ultimate symbol of the threat facing Jews. Israel stands as the guarantor of Jewish life and liberty worldwide.

However, physical survival is not seriously endangered in either America or Britain. What is at risk is neither life nor liberty but identity. The question is not 'Will we survive?' but '*How* will we survive?' As Jews? Or as something else, whose Jewish content will rapidly dissipate through the generations until nothing of it remains? We should not forget that physically, the lost ten tribes survived. They were merely lost to Jewish history. They chose to live as something other than as members of the people of Israel.

Survivalism answers no questions. It proposes no content for Jewish life other than life itself. In order to sustain even a minimally coherent view of why Jews should remain Jews rather than fade into anonymity, it has to postulate the darkest possible view of the human condition, namely (1) that Jews are uniquely singled out for persecution, (2) that they will remain so even if they marry out and merge into general society, and (3) that at times of danger they can rely on no other help than from themselves. For a generation waking to the trauma of the Holocaust at a time when Israel stood embattled and alone, these propositions seemed luminous in their certainty. It is doubtful in the extreme, however, whether any people can sustain itself on so negative a self-definition.

Traditionally, on Pesach, Jews solemnly acknowledged that 'It was not one alone who stood against us to destroy us; in every generation there have been those who stood against us to destroy us.' Collective Jewish memory begins in the book of Exodus with slavery and the threat of genocide. Yet, what follows is not survivalism but a declaration of faith. The story ends not with endurance but redemption. Liberation from Egypt leads on to righteous living, not merely to being alive. The Psalmist begins by saying, 'I will not die but live'. But he continues: 'and I will declare the works of God'.

What would Pesach be without its intimate connection with Shavuot? What would Israelite freedom be without the further festival of revelation? What would Jewish life have been without some content to inspire pride and purpose? Imagine the Bible as a narrative of mere survival. We would read about the Israelites becoming slaves in Egypt. We would thrill to the story of how they were led to freedom and to a land of their own. Then we would read about how they mingled and married with the local population and became as dead to the pages of world history as the ancient Jebusites and Perrizites. Could that conceivably be a story to inspire identification or belonging?

Survivalism has had its day. At a certain point in the evolution of modern Jewish consciousness it played a vital part, rousing Jews throughout the world to a full awareness of the epic nature of the events through which they had lived and in which one third of them had died. Future generations will look back on our days with awe and wonder, reflecting on how close the Jews came to extinction and how – toughened by the fires of hell on earth – they fought back to affirm life.

The post-war era, however, has now passed. It will live on eternally in Jewish memory. But it is not present Jewish reality. Israel is engaged in peace negotiations with its neighbours. The Jews of Eastern Europe are free to go on *aliyah*. Ethiopian Jewry has been rescued. Predictably, there will be moments of crisis in the future. We are not yet living at that time of universal peace for which we daily pray. Nevertheless, the period of high drama, in which the mere physical survival of the Jewish people hung in the balance, is over. Another challenge lies ahead. A new epoch has already begun. A third word must now enter and dominate the Jewish mind. The word, as will be clear from everything I have written thus far, is *continuity*.

THE HOLD OF THE PAST

Think of the figures listed in the last chapter for contributions to Jewish causes in 1991. They indicated that, communally, we allocated to education a fraction of what we gave to welfare and Israel. I suggested that these priorities make no sense at all. They go against Jewish principles and, in terms of the future of Anglo-Jewry, are little less than suicidal.

We can now understand them. In the age of integration, Jewish schools were largely unnecessary. In the Victorian era, institutions like the Jews' Free School in London, which in 1894 numbered 3,600 pupils, fulfilled an urgent function. They inducted the children of immigrants into British society. Once large-scale immigration ceased, so too did the *raison d'être* of such institutions. By 1939, the entire pupil population of Jewish day-schools in Britain had declined to 3,000. For the next generation, the cause of integration was best served by Jews attending British state or public schools, especially as they became less overtly Christian in character. Jewish education was delegated to a system of part-time, supplementary schooling: the *cheder* or *talmud torah*. Its second-class status was often painfully clear in terms of makeshift accommodation and teachers who were poorly qualified and even more poorly paid.

We are now long past that stage. The task of integration was accomplished with breathtaking speed and glittering success. For decades we have realised that the task now was not Anglicisation but Judaisation. Our children have often over-achieved as British citizens but under-achieved as Jews. None the less, habits of mind formed in the Victorian age have become deeply engrained in our attitudes and institutions. Our consistent under-spending on education stems directly from the age of integration, which no longer exists but still holds Anglo-Jewry captive in its sense of priorities.

In the age of survival, other priorities came to the fore: Israel and its wars, the rescue of Jewish communities endangered or oppressed, the Holocaust and how to understand it and perpetuate its victims' memory. Such issues dominated the agenda for twenty-five years, from 1967 to 1992. But as I have emphasised, *physical survival does not guarantee Jewish continuity*, least of all when that survival affects Jewries elsewhere, not here.

A whole generation of Anglo-Jews has grown up having learned the lesson that Jewishness is something that happens to someone else, somewhere else: in Germany, Austria and Poland in the 1930s, more recently in Russia, Ethiopia and above all in Israel. These are central chapters in modern Jewish history. Yet they do not explain what Jewishness means to me, here, now. They do not even explain what connects me as a Jew in Britain to these events and those people in other places and at other times. The proposition that 'all Jews are responsible for one another' is a religious one based on the idea of covenant. If I lack that idea and the religious vision of which it is a part, what sense am I to make of the bond that links me to people whose language I do not speak, whose history I do not know and whose aspirations I do not share?

Survivalism still dominates our community, and explains the massive disproportion between the funds we send Israel and those we devote to the Jewish needs of our own children. But with the *aliyah* of Ethiopian and Russian Jewry well under way and the changing political landscape in the Middle East, it is no longer the imperative of the hour. A new age has begun, and with it a quite new challenge.

FROM SURVIVAL TO CONTINUITY

An era is defined by what we cannot take for granted. The best indicator that times have changed comes when something that was simply not an issue for previous generations becomes urgent and problematic. The era of integration began when Jews who had hitherto led culturally enclosed lives were suddenly faced with the challenge of becoming part of another social order. The era of survival began when Jews, who had always known sporadic violence, were faced with the threat of cold, systematic annihilation. The era of continuity is about to begin with the realisation that the transmission of Jewish identity across the generations has become fragile and altogether at risk.

The difference between the three great epochs of modern Jewish history can be summarised simply. In the first, we were challenged to show that *a Jew can live as an Englishman or American*. In the second, we were challenged to show that *a Jew can live*. In the third, we are being challenged to show that *a Jew can live as a Jew*.

The move from survival to continuity will mean a fundamental shift in communal priorities. It will mean that as well as devoting our energies to saving Jewries abroad we will have to take on board the huge task of saving Jewry at home. It will mean that instead of taking Jewish identity for granted we will have to take it as something to be created. It will mean a momentous decision to engage in education and outreach in all its many forms and contexts on a scale never before attempted. It will mean building a community in which, in the words of Professor Isidore Twersky, every Jewish child and adult has the opportunity 'to be exposed to the mystery and romance of Jewish history, to the enthralling insights and special sensitivities of Jewish thought, to the sanctity and symbolism of Jewish existence, and to the power and profundity of Jewish faith'.

It can be done. Surveying the past two hundred years, one is awe-struck by the sheer power of the collective Jewish will once it has been mobilised. There were those who believed that integration was impossible and that the open society spelled the end of Judaism. There were others who believed that survival was impossible. Antisemitism, they believed, was inexorable and Zionism was doomed to fail. They were utterly wrong. Out of integration came a dazzling array of Jewish contributions to the economic, industrial, financial, academic, scientific, political and literary life of the West. Out of survival came the unique national renaissance of the State of Israel, barely fifty years after Theodor Herzl declared that 'If you will it, it is no dream.' If integration and survival proved possible, how much more so is continuity in a tolerant diaspora and in an age of Jewish sovereignty in Israel. Having passed every trial in our long and troubled history, it is unimaginable that we should fail the last: the trial that consists simply in this, *that there are no trials*.

Continuity can only be achieved, however, if we recognise that an era has passed and a new era begun. As we have seen, our priorities as reflected in the pattern of our charitable giving remain firmly locked in the past. They were right once, but they are wrong now. We have lived through two epochs which, from the perspective of Jewish history, have been utterly unprecedented. There was the wave of antisemitism throughout Europe in the 1880s, the mass migration of Jews to the west, the Holocaust, the birth of the State of Israel, Israel's wars of 1948, 1956, 1967, 1973 and 1982 and the great sequence of ingatherings culminating in Operation Moses and Operation Exodus. These were crises and emergencies in which the normal priorities of Jewish life were temporarily suspended. Now we must recover those priorities because, in the process, we neglected the Jewish future of our children, and we are beginning to pay the price.

There remains, though, a massive psychological barrier to be overcome. Possibly the most chilling words to have emerged from the entire American debate about Jewish continuity are these, by Dr Steven Bayme:

A survey done at Brandeis University of philanthropists who donate $100,000 or more to Jewish organisations discovered that no single issue so energised potential donors as the fear that their grandchildren would not be Jewish. However, the same survey indicated that these philanthropists were most reluctant to devote their funds to such an endeavour for *fear that nothing constructive could be done about it.*

Behind this fear are two presuppositions which have developed a tenacious hold in recent years, inducing paralysis where action is most needed. One is that only the ultra-Orthodox will survive as Jews. The other is that only Israelis will survive as Jews. If either or both of these assumptions is true, then for the majority of Jews today continuity will prove impossible. Nothing need be done, because nothing can be done. In fact, neither of these assumptions is valid, as I will now attempt to demonstrate.

7
Segregation?

'If you once saw someone cross a deep ravine while walking on a tightrope, would you or any of the many people watching him think to cross the high wire on your own because the tightrope walker is doing it?'

So asks a member of Jerusalem's ultra-Orthodox community in the course of Samuel Heilman's recent book, *Defenders of the Faith* (1992). He thereby issues the first great challenge to global Jewish continuity by questioning the attempt on the part of modern Jews to live in two worlds, Judaism and secular society. His view is that it cannot be done. Those who try to live in both worlds walk a tightrope, and most fall off. There are rare exceptions. But they are not, and cannot be, the rule.

Many observers take a dark view of the Jewish future. Noting the rising rates of intermarriage and disaffiliation, they have seen only one group resist these trends: the ultra-Orthodox. They alone have large families and minimal rates of defection. While other sections of Jewry have declined, they have increased in numbers. The reason is simple. While other Jews have *integrated* into secular society, the strictly Orthodox have *segregated*. They have built high walls against the world outside, and perhaps only those who do so are immune to assimilation. This suggests a pessimistic conclusion. *Whatever we do as a community, the majority of Jews will disappear*, leaving only the most committed. A strategy designed to address all Jews is bound to fail. Is this really so?

The challenge is a powerful one: any attempt to sustain Jewish identity while at the same time participating fully in a secular society is doomed to failure. Sooner or later, those who choose this route will find themselves or their children compromised by the culture around them. They will adopt, first its manners, then its values and eventually they will cease to be Jews. There is an iron law of assimilation, first articulated in the nineteenth century: the grandfather prays in Hebrew, the father prays in English, the son no longer prays, the grandson is no longer Jewish. There is only one way of avoiding this: *segregation*.

The proof is that those who have chosen the path of integration are now leaving the Jewish community at the rate of more than one in two, while segregated ultra-Orthodox communities are thriving, whether in

Manchester or Williamsburg, Bnei Brak or Jerusalem. A secular society is not a neutral society. It is deeply antithetical to Jewish values. It is sceptical of religious belief, authority and tradition. Its attitudes to marriage, adultery, promiscuity and homosexuality are profoundly un-Jewish. Jews who are open to the society around them are inevitably affected by it. As Jewish and secular values grow further apart, it becomes harder to stay Jewish. Sooner or later, Jewish integration leads to Jewish *dis*integration.

Only those who are willing to pay the price of segregation will survive as Jews, and, they argue, there are historical precedents to support their position. There have been many other instances of mass assimilation: the ten lost tribes, the wave of intermarriage which confronted Ezra and Nehemiah on their return from Babylon, the period of Hellenisation after Alexander the Great, and the forced conversions to Christianity and Islam in the Middle Ages. Indeed, Rashi, following rabbinic tradition, finds the phenomenon earlier still. The Torah says that the Israelites went up 'armed' [*hamushim*] out of Egypt. Rashi, however, gives an alternative translation: when the Israelites left Egypt they were 'reduced to a fifth'. Four-fifths of the people had become so acculturated that they refused to leave, and they perished in Egypt.

PRINCIPLED INTEGRATION

I respect this argument, but I cannot subscribe to it. Segregation is one path, but not the only path, to Jewish continuity.

At the very outset of emancipation, there were those who feared that social integration would lead to attrition in Jewish life. The late Yaakov Herzog once related this telling episode:

It is told of Baron Nathaniel Rothschild that, after winning his battle of many years to have the disabilities to members of the Jewish faith removed from the House of Lords, he slipped away from the hierarchy of Britain congratulating him on the achievement and was to be found prostrate in prayer in a small synagogue in the Whitechapel ghetto of East London, his lips murmuring, 'Would that this freedom shall not mean the diminution of our faith.'

Some nineteenth-century Torah sages, particularly in Eastern Europe, believed that the risks were simply too great. The ghetto had restricted Jews but preserved Judaism. Now that the walls were crumbling, the ghetto would have to be recreated in the form of voluntary close and closed Jewish communities: either Hasidic sects, grouped around a charismatic leader or Rebbe, or scholarly enclaves, built around *yeshivot*.

In Britain, France, Italy and Germany Jews responded differently. Emancipation seemed to them to be a mixed blessing, but a blessing none the less. They were aware of the dangers of integration but they knew also that it heralded the beginning of the end of the long exclusion of Jews from the life of the wider society, as aliens, outsiders or pariahs. Moreover, emancipation was a fact, and one which called for a religious advance, not a retreat. Such was the response of Chief Rabbi Nathan Adler in England and Rabbis Samson Raphael Hirsch and Azriel Hildesheimer in Germany. What Judaic insights lie behind the idea that segregation is not the only way?

First, as Samson Raphael Hirsch pointed out, exclusion from Western culture was not something Jews had chosen. It was something forced upon them. In all periods when they were allowed to participate in society, Jews did so. In talmudic times, there were sages who admired the Greeks for their astronomy, the Romans for their respect for parents and the Persians for their table manners. They said: 'If you are told that there is Torah among the nations, do not believe it. But if you are told that there is wisdom [*hokhmah*] among the nations, believe it.' Jews had and have a unique heritage: Torah and its way of life. But wisdom (the natural and human sciences) is universal. Maimonides admired Aristotle. Hirsch taught the Greek and Roman classics. Rabbi Soloveitchik wrote his doctorate on neo-Kantian metaphysics. One of Judaism's great insights is that there are two sources of knowledge, one which comes from Heaven through revelation, another which comes from earth through reason and the human imagination. When they conflict, the first takes precedence. But they do not always conflict. There is no greater testimony to the sages' love of knowledge from whatever source than that they coined a special blessing to be said on meeting great non-Jewish scholars.

Second, we have always believed that Jews are duty-bound to contribute to society as a whole. In his first words to Abraham, God said, 'through you, all the families of the earth shall be blessed'. When Jews were exiled in the days of Nebuchadnezzar, Jeremiah sent a letter urging them to 'Seek the peace of the city to which I have carried you into exile. Pray to the Lord for it, because if it prospers, you too will prosper.' Only rarely were they given the chance to enter into the mainstream of public life. When they were, they did so as conscientious citizens. Wherever they went, they enriched the life of the nation. Whenever they were expelled, the country concerned suffered a decline.

Thirdly, a religious principle is at stake. As Jews we are bidden to engage in *tikkun olam*, 'perfecting the world' under the sovereignty of God. Judaism is not a world-denying faith. We believe that we are commanded to become 'partners with the Holy One, blessed be He, in the work of creation'. Human dignity, wrote Rabbi Soloveitchik, consists in 'man's capability of dominating his environment and exercising control over it'. When we help to make society's laws more just, its economy more productive, its education more intense, its medicine more effective and its welfare more humane, these are not religiously neutral acts. They are part of the Torah's imperative to perfect society as the arena of righteousness and justice.

Fourthly, the Torah itself is concerned with the impact Jews make on the world around them. At the end of his life, Moses told the Israelites: 'Observe [the laws of the Torah] carefully, for this will show your wisdom and understanding to the nations, who will say, "Surely this great nation is a wise and understanding people."' Whether or not there is a Jewish 'mission' to the world, there is certainly a Jewish responsibility to act in an admirable and exemplary fashion. This idea is at the heart of Judaism's two great concepts of *kiddush ha-Shem* and *hillul ha-Shem*, the sanctification and desecration of God's name. Jews have undertaken to be, in Isaiah's phrase, God's witnesses. When they are admired, that is a sanctification. When they are justly criticised, that is a desecration. Samson Raphael Hirsch rightly sensed that Enlightenment, despite its many risks, opened the way for a new admiration for Judaism among non-Jews. It duly came: from Goethe, George Eliot and Tolstoy. Even their bitterest critic, Nietzsche, could write that Europe owes to Jews, 'the grand style in morality, the fearfulness and majesty of infinite demands'.

Last but by no means least, the open society was *where Jews were*. The Torah is given to Jews where they are, at all places and times. The sages emphasised that 'the Torah was not given to the ministering angels', meaning that it was meant not for utopia but for the real world with its conflicts and temptations. The majority, by choosing integration, had not rejected Judaism. Therefore Judaism could not reject them. Samson Raphael Hirsch once asked whom Abraham might have had in mind when he asked God to spare Sodom if it contained ten righteous people? What would it have been like to be righteous in such a corrupt civilisation? He answered that such a person would not be 'one who keeps to his own four walls'. He would instead be one who 'is to be found "in the midst of the city" and in lively connection with everything and everybody'. Even in Sodom, to be righteous is not to be segregated. It is to be a participant in society, challenging it where it needs to be challenged, but not abandoning it.

So in the East religious Jews chose segregation, while in the West they chose integration. More than a century has passed. We can now ask with hindsight: Which side was right? And what was at stake in the argument?

THE GERMAN EXPERIENCE

Segregation is a counsel of despair, a strategy of last resort. The Torah sages were correct in their assessment of Central and Eastern Europe. More perceptively than their liberal contemporaries, they saw that for all their enlightened rhetoric, the societies around them were hostile. They were demanding the virtual dismemberment of Judaism and offering only the semblance, not the reality, of tolerance in return. Antisemitism exploded in Russia in the 1880s, sending millions of Jews into flight. Integration had never been a real possibility.

But Chief Rabbi Adler and Sir Moses Montefiore were also correct in their judgement of England. In the Middle Ages it had been the first country to mount a Blood Libel and the first to expel its Jews. But modern England was a place of genuine tolerance. In 1837, Montefiore wrote in his diary: 'I am most firmly resolved not to give up the smallest part of our religious forms and privileges to obtain civil rights.' But he suspected that he would not have to, and he was right. Adler, for his part, believed that if halakhic Judaism were projected in a dignified and decorous manner, it would retain the allegiance of most Jews, and virtually to the present day he has been proved right as well.

One sage, however, was proven wrong, and that single failure has loomed disproportionately large in the minds of post-Holocaust Jewry. The most passionate exponent of integration was Samson Raphael Hirsch. His great work was achieved in Oldenburg, Moravia and Frankfurt between the 1830s and the 1860s. Hirsch could not have foreseen that Germany – the birthplace of Lessing, Schiller, Goethe and Kant – should become in the 1870s the source of racial antisemitism and in the 1940s the perpetrator of the greatest crime ever committed against humanity.

German–Jewish integration ended in Auschwitz, and we are still living with the trauma engendered by that fact. It has convinced many Jews, in Israel and outside, that the gentile world is incurably hostile to everything Judaism represents. There is no possibility or point in trying to live in the larger stream of human civilisation, for it has proved to be neither human nor civilised. The best we can do is to withdraw into our citadels of the heart and the mind – the Hasidic sect or the *yeshiva* – and wait, if necessary for centuries, for better times. Then, perhaps, we can emerge, but not before, and certainly not now.

It is this fact more than any other which has lent immense power to the Jewish segregationist vision of the world. Let us recall that it is only in recent times that ultra-Orthodoxy has been triumphalist. Before the Holocaust, its own most fervent protagonists believed that they were fighting a desperate and losing battle. The greatest of them all, the *Hafetz Hayyim* (Rabbi Israel Meir Kagan, 1838–1933), wrote in 1930: 'The sanctity of the Holy Torah is declining from day to day at a frightening pace. The new generation is growing up without Torah and faith. They are becoming wayward children who deny God and His Torah. And if, God forbid, this situation continues much longer, who knows to what condition we will fall.'

After the Second World War the Enlightenment was called into question, not only by Jews but by non-Jews as well. Political emancipation had led to antisemitism on a scale never before witnessed. High civilisation had singularly failed to civilise. Kantian ethics was powerless in the face of attempted genocide. Science has proved to be not the dreamed-of answer but the nightmare problem: from nuclear destruction to environmental damage to genetic manipulation. Robert Bellah, one of the great social commentators of our time, notes that 'Progress, modernity's master idea, seems less compelling when it appears that it may be progress into the abyss.' That is precisely the segregationist case.

Yet, in the final analysis, such a view is simply too pessimistic. Rabbi Adin Steinsaltz, the great talmudist, once declared his belief that 'This is the worst possible world *in which there is still hope*.' In that marvellously rabbinic aphorism lies the clue to the mainstream (though not the only) Judaic vision of history. Things *are* bad. But they are not unredeemable. Antisemitism exists. But so does philosemitism. There are aspects of contemporary culture that are pagan and destructive. But there are others that inspire individuals to rediscover faith and the religious life. To see only the bad but not the good in what is around us is neither Judaic nor even realistic. It is the safe option to insulate ourselves from all contact with the outside world. But when has Judaism ever been the safe option?

Faith involves risk and courage. A *midrash* contains a most profound commentary on the act of creation. It interprets the phrase, 'the God of faith' as 'God who had *faith in the world He was about to create*'. In creation, God gave humanity freewill. Ever since, the world has been a place of conflict, violence and injustice. Yet, God took the risk that from human freewill would emerge not only bad but good, not only injustice but compassion, not only war but peace. That was God's faith, and it is ours.

The segregationist who spoke to Samuel Heilman was correct. To attempt to live as a Jew in the secular world is like walking a tightrope. However, Rabbi Nachman of Bratslav saw that this was the inescapable condition of human existence as such. 'Know,' he said, 'that a person walks in life on a very narrow bridge. The most important rule is never to be afraid.'

A JEW IN THE STREET

The argument between integrationists and segregationists, though it lives on, belongs essentially to an age that has passed. The structure of society has changed. In the first half of the nineteenth century, when Hirsch was championing integration and the sages to the East were opposing it, European culture was still strongly Christian. To acculturate, Jews had at least partially to assimilate. Heinrich Heine felt the need to convert. So did Moses Mendelssohn's children. So too did Gustav Mahler. Today, Western societies are pluralist, in fact and in principle. What Hirsch could only dream of is now reality. Jews participate in all political, ethical and cultural processes as equal members. So, more significantly, does Judaism itself.

The nineteenth-century equation was: 'Be a Jew at home and a man in the street.' Some believed that Judaism could survive on these terms, others did not. Thus the argument, 'Integrate or segregate', was born. Today, when every other religious or ethnic group wears its badges of identity openly, the challenge is to be a Jew at home *and* in the street.

There has never been a time when Judaic virtues have been more admired by society as a whole. We are envied for our strong community life, our family traditions, our passion for education, our commitment to welfare. We are praised for our charity, our individual achievements and our collective energy. Our views are sought on social, medical and business ethics. If ever there was a time when Jews could feel confident that they have something unique to contribute to the common good, it is now. What a tragedy it is that at the very time when others are turning to our teachings, we ourselves are deserting them.

The challenge to contemporary Jewry is not *segregation* but *education*. We believe that we live in two worlds. But we do not. We live in one: the world of secular culture. The overwhelming majority of Jews in today's diaspora know history but not Jewish history. They know literature, but not Jewish literature. They discuss ethics but not Jewish ethics. They know other languages, but not Hebrew.

We have made a fateful error, one which every historical instinct should have guarded us against. We believed that Jewish identity could be sustained in an open society by occasional gestures of affiliation: attending synagogue on High Holidays, contributing to Jewish charities and eating ethnic Jewish food. Jewish identity, we believed, is something like English or American identity: given, taken for granted, and not in constant need of expression or reinforcement.

It was Matthew Arnold, that great Victorian moralist, who most clearly saw that what was unique to Judaism was its insistence on translating identity into action. 'No people,' he wrote, 'ever felt so strongly as the people of the Old Testament, the Hebrew people, that conduct is three-fourths of our life and its largest concern.' In the thirteenth century the *Sefer Ha-Hinnukh* expressed the same truth in slightly different words: 'The heart is drawn after the deed.' That is one of the central truths of Torah and *halakhah*. We are what we do. To be a Jew requires an ongoing programme of Jewish learning and Jewish doing. Without this, our Jewish consciousness atrophies, our Jewish pulse grows weak. It revives at times of crisis. But no one who is truly alive needs a crisis to convince him that he is alive.

The Judaic challenge of the open society has not ended. It has hardly yet begun. We have mastered the art of being Britons in Britain, Americans in America. Yet, we have not yet mastered the art of being Jews in the public domain. The Jewish public presence tends to be either anonymous or self-critical. Today, when Jewish intellectuals speak, they are more likely to attack Judaism than to expound it, to criticise Israel than to defend it. Of no other faith community is this true. Nor do they speak with any knowledge of what they dismiss. I once remonstrated with a leading Jewish intellectual, a polymath who has written distinguished books on literacy, language and translation. I asked him how in intellectual integrity he could be literate in every culture but his own and be fluent in half-a-dozen languages but unable to read Hebrew. I had taken the trouble to read each of his books. Why had he not taken the trouble to read Jewish books? He did not reply. The question remains unanswered.

The challenge is education. We have paid a painful price for two centuries of alienation between Judaism and many of the finest Jewish minds. Halakhic scholarship has continued to thrive, but essential areas of Jewish thought remain in their infancy. We know the rules governing relationships between Jew and Jew, but our understanding of relationships between Jew and non-Jew in a plural and interdependent world is far from clear. Only recently have scholars begun to evolve Judaic responses to macro-economic, political, environmental and scientific questions.

The consequence is that we have an artificially narrow sense of what constitutes a Jewish deed. We know that going to synagogue or keeping *kashrut* is Jewish. Yet, we are not sure that there is a Judaic way of being an academic or a journalist or an artist or an architect or a politician. When Jews speak as Jews in the public arena, they often confuse Jewish self-interests (or the general interests of minorities) with Judaic principle. Nor, ironically, is it any different in Israel. There, the religious voice is identified with sectarian politics and sectional self-interest rather than societal ideals in the tradition of the prophets and the sages.

Never has living Jewishly in an open society been more possible, more rewarding and less demanding of assimilation. For it to succeed, though, a Jew must know what it is to be a Jew. Our grandparents knew, but they had to learn what it was to be an Englishman or American. We know what they did not. But we do not know what they knew, and we must make sure that we and our children learn.

It is not true to say that living in two worlds has failed. It is fairer to say that it has not seriously been tried.

NEW CHALLENGES

Segregationist Jewry lives under the shadow of the Holocaust, by which it was almost destroyed. For the past fifty years its imperative has been survival, and it has achieved little less than a miracle. It has rebuilt Hungary in Williamsburg, Lithuania in Bnei Brak and Jerusalem. But time moves on, and challenges change.

Integration and survival were extreme reactions to exceptional circumstances. The one involved too little attention to Judaism, the other too little to the world outside. The coming era will pose problems for both sides. Integrationists face the challenge of recapturing a compelling sense of the Jewish mind and deed. The segregationists, too, will face dilemmas. They already do. Their communities have grown too large to be self-supporting. They have already been touched by the consumer ethic and by divorce. In Israel they have entered the political arena. Ironically, each side has expertise the other needs. Much will depend on whether the relationship between them is one of dialogue or confrontation.

Far from being the sole survivors, ultra-Orthodox Jews have an essential role to play in the continuity of the Jewish people as a whole. Like the *cohanim* of biblical times, they form a religious elite within Jewry. Like them, they spend their days in the precincts of the holy while others engage with the world. Relations between the priests and the rest of Israel were sometimes strained in biblical times. So too are relations between the ultra-Orthodox and the rest of the Jewish world today. Nevertheless the ideal was set out by the prophet Malachi: 'The lips of a priest guard knowledge, and from his mouth men should seek instruction'. That remains the intriguing possibility.

Whenever the *yeshiva* and Hasidic communities have attempted this role they have met with success. In the past quarter-century, they have been Jewry's greatest practitioners of outreach. They have revitalised dying congregations and created centres of Jewish learning where none existed. They bring to Jewish continuity what it most needs: Judaism as an intense and total experience. Theirs cannot be the way of all Jews, any more than the life of the *cohen* was the way of all Israel in Bible times. Relations between them and the rest of Jewry will continue to be tense. But there is great potential for cooperation if both sides can lessen their suspicion of each other.

The segregationist challenge to global Jewish continuity is mistaken. Jews are leaving the Jewish people today not because they are involved in society but because they are *un*involved in Judaism. This is not because they have rejected religion, but because they have never learned its complexities, as difficult for the untutored ear to understand as the late quartets of Beethoven, but surely, at the very least, as rewarding.

Samuel Heilman, one of the most perceptive of contemporary Jewish observers, comments at the end of his study of ultra-Orthodox

Jewry: 'Their extraordinary success in surviving and growing, in holding on to their children, must make the rest of us take notice.'

The segregationists succeed not because they are segregated, but because they adopt precisely the strategy I have advocated in this book. They put the Jewish needs of their children first. They build schools and intensive Jewish communities. They make education their first priority and deepest love. If they, who live secluded from secular society, feel the need to do so, can we who have chosen to live in the heart of society, do less? Certainly we need it more.

8
Israel and the Diaspora

In May 1993 the new President of Israel, Ezer Weizman, made a speech which created a brief flurry of controversy. It was Jerusalem Day, and he was addressing leaders from Jewish communities throughout the world. They had come expecting a conventional address about the centrality of Jerusalem to Jews worldwide. Instead they were subjected to an assault against the very concept of the continued diaspora itself. He urged 'The future of the Jews is in Israel,' and continued: 'We know what mixed marriages can bring. From a demographic point of view, Israel is the only place. I urge you to make Israel your home.'

This is the second great challenge to my thesis, and on the face of it, it is as powerful as the segregationist argument. In the spirit of Ezer Weizman a critic might argue as follows:

I grant everything you say about the crisis facing the diaspora. Assimilation is rife. Mixed marriage is rising. The Jewish family is fragile. Jewish identity is becoming weaker and confused. The Jewish future is altogether in doubt. You have diagnosed the symptoms correctly. But the cure you have prescribed is wrong.

You have spoken about Jewish continuity in the diaspora and you are about to say how it is to be achieved. But whatever you say next will be mistaken because it proceeds from a mistaken premise. *There can be no Jewish continuity in the diaspora.* Wherever Jews are, outside Israel, they are a minority. Even in the United States, the world's largest Jewish community, they form no more than two per cent of the population. The invariable rule is that minorities disappear. Not immediately, but ultimately. That is true even of Jews, the world's great survivors. The latest figures prove it. Wherever you turn – Britain, France, Italy, Scandinavia, the United States, South America – Jewish communities are on the wane. They are assimilating, declining and slowly disappearing. That is a process you cannot reverse.

Nor is it a process you should *wish* to reverse, because the State of Israel is more than a fact. It is a value. Israel is the one place where Jewish continuity *can* be achieved. No less importantly, it is also the one place where Jewish continuity *should* be achieved. Israel is our home, our birthplace and our identity. We lost it for nineteen hundred years. We have recovered it now. Our ancestors prayed for the chance to be 'Next year in Jerusalem.' Today, we have the opportunity to be '*This* year in Jerusalem.' Whether we are religious or secular Jews, whether we are moved by Jewish faith or Jewish culture or Jewish history, Israel is the only place where we belong.

Your talk about Jewish continuity in the diaspora is thus at best an irrelevance, at worst a serious distraction from the task of our time, namely encouraging *aliyah*, the return of the Jews to Israel. Whatever you do, you will fail. The rate of attrition will continue to rise. Diaspora communities will continue to decline. You will do worse than fail. You will shift attention from Israel, which is where our future lies. You will endanger the land, the state and its people. You will deprive it of potentional funds. You will rob it of *olim*, of the immigrants it needs. You will have encouraged Jews to stay in the diaspora in the illusion that there can be a future in the diaspora. President Weizman was right. The best thing Jews outside Israel can do, for themselves, for Israel and for the sake of the Jewish people, is to leave.

THE ISRAEL OF SURVIVAL

No argument more perfectly encapsulates my thesis than this. I have argued that we are entering a new era in modern Jewish history. A new era calls for a new way of thinking, a paradigm shift. Attitudes that were appropriate to one age may become inappropriate, dysfunctional, in the next. The world changes. Nothing is as it was. At some stage even those – *especially* those – whose values are eternal must pause to look at the compass and take new bearings. That is true now. And nowhere is it more true than in our thinking about Israel.

My hypothetical critic is locked into a particular era and its mindset, the era of *survival*. It began in the mid-nineteenth century with the first stirrings of what we now call Zionism. It reached a series of peaks as crisis after crisis struck the Jewish world: first the Russian pogroms of the 1880s, then the Dreyfus affair in the 1890s, then the First World War, then the earthquake of the Holocaust and the birth of the State of Israel. The tremors continued through Israel's wars of 1967 and 1973, the rise of international anti-Zionism, and the dramatic migration of Jews from the Arab world, Eastern Europe and Ethiopia. During the whole of this period, the Jewish world was dominated by a single ultimate question: *where can Jews live?*.

Survival still dominates our thinking, and with it a particular view of the place of Israel in Jewish life. Israel means many different things to different Jews. For some, it is the place for Jews to be religious. For others, it is the place where they can be secular. For some, it is where they can be most intensely conscious of being Jewish. For others, it is the one place in the world where they can be Jewish *without* being self-conscious. Every ideology, theology or philosophy of Jewish life today has its own distinctive vision of the land and state of Israel, and no two perspectives are alike. Only one thing connects them all. *Israel is the place of Jewish survival.* This is the Israel which unites Jews throughout the world. It is the Israel to which we turn in dedication and pride. It is the Israel which has rescued the Jewish people – all Jews, everywhere – from homelessness and powerlessness in the century of antisemitism and the Final Solution. It is the Israel which has given Jews a vestige of security in a dangerously insecure world.

But *the role of Israel in an era of continuity is not the same as in an era of survival.* The land is the same. The people are the same. But the age and its challenges have changed. In the future, Israel will be no less central to our lives. But its relationship to the diaspora, and the diaspora's relationship to it, must undergo a transformation. If not, we will be held captive by attitudes that were right then but wrong now. We will make bad decisions, decisions that will harm Israel, the diaspora and the relationship between them.

NEGATION OF THE DIASPORA

The sentiment to which President Weizman was giving expression has a name: *shelilat ha-golah*, 'negation of the diaspora'. Far from being a new idea, it is the oldest of all Zionist ideologies. As a concept, it has its origins over a century ago.

Zionism – the Jewish national movement – was born in the nineteenth century. It grew out of a complex set of influences. There was the impact of European nationalism on thinkers such as Rabbi Zvi Hirsch Kalischer. If the Italians, Poles and Hungarians could achieve independence, why not the Jews? There was the sense of messianic possibility, brought about by the modern era, which moved Rabbi Yehuda Alkalai. And underlying virtually every form of Zionism, religious or secular, was the biblical idea of exile and return, the ingathering of Jews to the promised land. Undoubtedly, however, the most potent factor in the development of modern political Zionism was a sense of the *failure of integration*, a growing intuition that emancipation was going badly wrong.

It began with the Damascus blood libel of 1840. The realisation that this medieval antisemitic myth was still potent in an age of supposed enlightenment shook both Alkalai and Moses Hess and launched them on an intellectual journey which ended in the conclusion that only in their own land, responsible for their own fate, could Jews be safe. The Russian pogroms of 1881 had a similar effect on Yehuda Leib Pinsker. The Dreyfus affair in France in 1894 reinforced the same conviction in Theodor Herzl. Western Jews had hoped that through Enlightenment and emancipation the doors of European society would be opened to them. Yet, at the same time anti-Jewish prejudice was stimulated to new and virulent forms. Throughout Europe Jews became 'the Jewish problem'. To the more far-sighted, it became clear that in many countries integration would be worse than painful. It would be impossible.

Herzl put it bluntly in *The Jewish State* (1896):

> We have sincerely tried everywhere to merge with the national communities in which we live, seeking only to preserve the faith of our fathers. It is not permitted us. In vain are we loyal patriots, sometimes superloyal; in vain do we make the same sacrifices of life and property as our fellow citizens; in vain do we strive to enhance the fame of our native lands in the arts and sciences, or her wealth by trade or commerce. In our native lands where we have lived for centuries we are still decried as aliens, often by men whose ancestors had not yet come at a time when Jewish sighs had long been heard in the country.

Whatever the positive aspirations of the early Zionists, and they were many, the underlying proposition which drove the movement was a negative one: *shelilat ha-golah*, the negation of the diaspora as an environment in which to create a Jewish future.

This negation took many forms. There were those like Hess, Pinsker, Herzl and Nordau, who saw it mainly in terms of anti-semitism. Jews were an unassimilable minority who in European society would always be the first target of hatred. There were others, like Jacob Klatzkin, who on the contrary held that assimilation was all too possible. Religion had preserved Jewish identity in the past, but its hold was rapidly waning, and now only the secular bases of land and language were capable of preserving Jews as a nation. Others focused on the economic or cultural dimension. Only in their own land could Jews forge an autonomous society and thus put an end to their condition of marginality and alienation. Rabbi Avraham Kook saw the issue as a spiritual one. Exile had gone on too long. It had created an unnatural split between body and soul. After centuries in the ghetto, Jews had turned in upon themselves and lost the living connection between religion, land and language. 'Jewish original creativity,' he wrote, 'is impossible except in the land of Israel.'

The Zionist case was not readily accepted. We tend to forget how bitterly the battle was waged between Zionism and its Jewish opponents. When Theodor Herzl convened the first Zionist Congress in 1897, he originally intended to hold it in Munich. The German Orthodox and Reform rabbinate, otherwise deeply divided, came together in a unique joint declaration dissociating themselves from the project for a Jewish national home, and succeeded in having the Congress banned from Germany. It was held instead in Basle, Switzerland. Even in the 1930s and 1940s, many of the leading representatives of Anglo-Jewry remained anti-Zionist and made representations to this effect to the British government. It was not until 1939, with the election of Selig Brodetsky as President, and 1943 with the dissolution of the non-Zionist Joint Foreign Committee, that Zionism finally prevailed in the Board of Deputies.

Throughout this period, one of the most fraught in Jewish history, the argument was conducted in either-or terms: Israel *or* the diaspora, integration *or* survival. In part the debate turned on the mixed signals Europe delivered to Jews. On the one hand, there was the message of emancipation: toleration, civil liberties and an open society. On the other, there was the message of antisemitism: intolerance, prejudice and persecution. Equally, however, the controversy turned on the question of Jewish identity. Was it essentially *religious* or *national*? If it was religious, Jews did not need a state. If it was national, Jews did not need a diaspora. The clash of ideologies was fierce. Each side tended to negate the other and to portray its adherents in terms of unflattering stereotypes.

The argument came to an end in 1967. The Holocaust revealed the terrible, ultimately unbearable, cost of Jewish homelessness. The State of Israel was the one guarantee of safety for Jews wherever they might live. A threat to it was a threat to every Jew. In one of the formative events of modern Jewish history, the Six Day War placed Israel at the centre of Jewish consciousness, and it has remained there ever since. In an age dominated by the spectre of genocide, Israel was and is the guarantor of Jewish survival.

Not surprisingly, therefore, *shelilat ha-golah* has remained the dominant Israeli view of the diaspora, given expression by such varied thinkers as Gershom Scholem, Natan Rotenstreich, Eliezer Schweid and Rabbi Zvi Yehuda Kook. It has been lent enormous weight by three factors: the Holocaust (which A.B. Yehoshua described as the 'final decisive refutation' of diaspora existence), the rise of antisemitism in Central and Eastern Europe, and the continued demographic erosion of the diaspora. Taken together, they seemed to confirm the classic thesis of Zionism: that the diaspora is threatened equally by cruelty and kindness, the former leading to annihilation, the latter to assimilation. In his survey, *Galut* (1986), Arnold Eisen could conclude that 'Negation of the diaspora . . . stands at the very centre of contemporary Zionist reflection'.

It is my contention, however, that we are entering a new era in Jewish life, one that will pose quite different challenges than the age of survival. Negation of the diaspora made sense when what was at stake was *pikuach nefesh*, the saving of Jewish lives. When a house is on fire, what matters is bringing its inhabitants to safety, not a nuanced philosophy of Jewish life. *Shelilat ha-golah*, born over a century ago, had a vital part to play in alerting Jews to the dangers that lay in store for them in Europe. It mobilised the formidable energies necessary for the tasks of ingathering Jews, building the land and creating a state.

As an ideology it has persisted, virtually unchanged, until the present day. In the meantime, however, the whole of Jewish life has been transformed. The centre of the diaspora is no longer in Europe but America. The State of Israel is not a dream but a forty-five-year-old reality. A momentous phase in Jewish history, the most dramatic since the destruction of the second Temple, has been enacted. Yet we have not yet fully adjusted to the significance of the events that have taken place. To a remarkable degree, when we speak about Israel and the diaspora, whether we do so *in* Israel or the diaspora, we do so in terms drawn from the 1890s, not the 1990s. That is why we find it difficult to think lucidly about either. We are living in one time-zone while our minds are in another. We live in the era of continuity. But our thinking remains trapped in the era of survival.

THE EFFECT OF ISRAEL ON THE DIASPORA

A century after the idea of *shelilat ha golah* was born, what has actually happened? Much of Zionist prediction has come true, but as much has not. The reason is not that the prediction itself was false. It is that the existence of the State of Israel has changed the equation. It was one thing to talk about the diaspora in the days when there was no Jewish state. It is quite another to talk about it when there is.

The most obviously unexpected phenomenon is that the diaspora still exists. Jews did not do what Arthur Koestler recommended in 1948 and what Herzl had predicted half a century before: either go to Israel and live as Jews or stay in the diaspora and assimilate. The vast majority of Jews stayed in the diaspora and continued to live as Jews. Paradoxically, this was due in no small measure to Israel itself. By making it safe to live in Israel, the state made it safe *not* to live in Israel. Israel became the home of every Jew, in the sense of the famous line of the poet Robert Frost: 'Home is the place where, when you have to go there, they have to take you in.' Israel, by being 'the city of refuge', made it safer to be a Jew anywhere in the world. Far from negating the diaspora, Israel made a post-Holocaust diaspora possible.

Israel invigorated the western diaspora in other ways as well. Activism and fund-raising on its behalf created new forms of Jewish involvement. From the Soviet Union to America, Jews were touched by the drama of Israel's wars and daring rescues. Israel awoke slumbering identities. It gave Jews throughout the world vicarious pride. The growth of Israeli *yeshivot* in the 1960s, often established by rabbis from the diaspora, gave momentum to a worldwide religious revival. The renaissance of Jewish scholarship in Israeli universities gave rise to similar movements in America and elsewhere. Hebrew began to replace Yiddish and Ladino as the international language of Jews. Israeli art and music gave new life to Jewish culture outside Israel. If Israel has brought a new confidence and vigour to Jewish life, it has done so not for itself alone but for Jews throughout the world. In a second paradoxical development, Israel made the *golah* seem less like *galut*, the 'diaspora' less like 'exile'.

There were other less positive phenomena which further confounded the black-and-white of ideology. Contrary to Herzl's hopes, the existence of Israel did not end antisemitism. It created a new form, anti-Zionism, directed not only against Israel but against Jews in the diaspora, seen collectively as Israel's allies. Nor has Jewish migration proved to be a one-way street. For some time now, as many Jews have left Israel through *yeridah* as have come to Israel through *aliyah*. Nor has Israel solved the problem of Jewish identity as religious, secular and cultural Zionists thought it would. The clash of tradition and modernity is as sharp in Israel as in the diaspora, indeed more so. The idea of an 'autonomous' Jewish culture has, in any case, proved to be an illusion. Israel in its way is as influenced by western secularism as are the diaspora communities of the West. *No* open society has an autonomous culture in an age of international communications.

So Israel and the diaspora have interacted in unexpected and sometimes paradoxical ways. What we can say with some confidence is that an era is drawing to its close, an era marked by the Holocaust, the birth of the State, and the rescue of threatened diaspora communities. The Jewish map has been transformed. One Jewry after another has been transported to Israel: refugees from Eastern Europe, Nazi Germany, Bulgaria, Rumania, Iraq, Iran, Yemen, Syria, Ethiopia, the former Soviet Union and the Balkans. The diaspora communities that remain are, for the most part, free of immediate fear of unrest and persecution. Israel may face danger in the future. So may Jews in the diaspora. Yet the great drama of survival has, one hopes, passed its peak. Israel has turned to negotiations for peace with its Arab neighbours. The diaspora is turning to its domestic crisis of continuity. For the foreseeable future the dominant question is likely to be, not *where* can Jews live, but *how* shall Jews live.

TWO OPTIONS FOR THE FUTURE

In some form or another, then, the diaspora is likely to persist into the foreseeable future. It represents some nine million out of world Jewry's total population of 13 million. It is centred in countries where, in the main, antisemitism is unlikely in the near future to provoke mass migration. What then is the most appropriate policy to be adopted towards this diaspora in terms of the future of the Jewish people?

Broadly speaking, there are three possible alternatives. First, there is the policy that has been in evidence in Anglo-Jewry until now. The majority of the community funds are sent to Israel. Curiously, this policy is indicative of *shelilat ha-golah*, negation of the diaspora, internalised by a diaspora community itself.

The logic of such a position may never be consciously articulated. Nevertheless we can imagine the line of thought that lies behind it: 'The future of Anglo-Jewry is in doubt. I do not know whether my children will marry Jews or non-Jews. I do not know whether I will have Jewish grandchildren. In any case, nothing I can do will make any difference. Living as we do as a minority in an open society, we cannot survive in the long run as Jews. Only in Israel is the Jewish future safe. Therefore I must help to build Israel. If my family cannot survive *personally* here they will survive *vicariously* there. Israel is where Jews survive.'

The second option, and one which may become more common in

the future, is to devote the whole of a community's funds to its own interests. The logic here is the reverse of the first position: 'Israel once needed the help of the diaspora, but no longer. It is forty-five years old, a mature country with an expanding economy. Its defence and infrastructure needs are best met by other governments, most notably by that of the United States, which will continue to support Israel not because of the "Jewish lobby" but because it is in its own best interest to have a democratic pro-western ally in a Middle East increasingly dominated by Islamic fundamentalism. Israel will continue to enjoy the friendship, but no longer needs the financial support, of Jewries elsewhere.'

'It is time to recognise that Israel and the diaspora are two different answers to the question: what is it to be a Jew? Israel is the national answer: to be a Jew is to live in a Jewish state. The diaspora is the religious answer: to be a Jew is to live by the Jewish faith anywhere in the world. The diaspora has done its duty by Israel. It has supported it through its early struggles. The time has now come for us to go our separate ways. Israel does not answer the question of how to be a Jew in Britain any more than Britain answers the question of how to be a Jew in Israel. We must now return to our primary task, of being British by nationality and Jewish by religion. We have built Israel for long enough. We must now concentrate on building ourselves.'

By now we recognise these respective positions. They come from the mind-sets of survival on the one hand, and integration on the other. There is a clear conflict of interests between them. However, and less obviously, they are both recipes for disaster.

The first policy is bound to hasten the very collapse it predicts. If the diaspora refuses to take its own future seriously, it will have no future. It will have created a structure in which Jewish education, experience and life take place not here but there, not in London but in Jerusalem. Nor will its children necessarily live in Jerusalem. The ironic experience of the Jewish community in South Africa has been that, having created a powerful structure of Zionist day-schools, the vast majority of its children have left the country not for Israel but for Australia, Canada and Britain. In short, a community which directs its energies to Israel at the cost of neglecting itself will find that it has sacrificed its children for the sake of Israel when such a sacrifice was neither necessary nor helpful to Israel.

The second policy is equally short-sighted. For centuries, the most powerful barrier Jews had against assimilation was the knowledge that, ultimately, home was elsewhere. On Pesach they re-enacted the exodus from Egypt. On Sukkot they recalled that outside Israel the most secure house was only a temporary dwelling. They never forgot that the Jewish people had a land and language of its own. Judaism was more than a faith. It was the code of a nation, and a nation has a home. Jews were exemplary citizens of the societies in which they lived. Yet, in a deep, metaphysical, even messianic sense, home was somewhere else. They were on a journey, as Jews since the time of Abraham have been on a journey. Therefore they could never say, even of Poland where they lived for eight hundred years, or Babylon–Iraq where they lived for two thousand years, here my descendants will stay for ever.

Jewish life cannot be sustained without Israel at its core. That was true for the nineteen hundred years when there was no Jewish state. It is no less true now that the state exists. One of the most profound turning points in the history of a community is when it declares that it has no interest in the return to Zion. That occurred among Reform Jews in nineteenth-century Germany. Similarly, there are people today who claim that twentieth-century America is not *galut*. It has none of the characteristics of exile. Jews are equal, respected and secure. They identify with the American dream. Indeed Jews have been the authors of some of its most famous expressions. The inscription under the Statue of Liberty was written by Emma Lazarus. Irving Berlin wrote 'God bless America'. As Israel is to Israeli Jews, so America is to American Jews: home.

Sooner or later, such a view spells the end of Jewish life. To be a Jew means to live between two worlds: the finite and the infinite, the particular and the universal, here and elsewhere. Once that tension is broken, the dissolution of Jewish identity follows as inevitably as night follows day. The process takes on average four generations. But it is inexorable. A diaspora that turns in upon itself and severs its connection with Israel is a community which, wittingly or otherwise, is breaking its links with Jewish tradition and the Jewish people and taking the first step on the path to complete assimilation.

FROM CONFLICT TO CONVERGENCE

There is a third option: the option of continuity. To understand it we must grasp what has changed in Jewish life. Israel and the diaspora once represented radically different versions of Jewish identity. One was national and collective. The other was religious and individual.

For a century, as we have seen, this either-or was the subject of fierce ideological debate between the two camps. To be sure, there were exceptions on both sides. There were those, like Simon Dubnow, who believed that Jews could create a collective life outside Israel through self-rule in Eastern Europe. There were others, like Rabbi Isaac Reines, who preached religious Zionism. Such examples were nevertheless exceptions. For the majority of Jews there was a clear distinction: Zionism was one expression of Jewish life, the diaspora was another. There was no point of contact between the two.

Today, however, Israel and the diaspora have grown more, not less, alike. On the one hand, Israel by its very existence has given the diaspora a collective dimension. It has united Jews worldwide as never before, given them a joint focus, shared experiences, and even a new international language, *Ivrit*. If today we can talk of a single Jewish people, the reason is Israel.

At the same time, Israel itself has become less collectivist since the time when the *kibbutz* symbolised the Zionist dream. It has moved – as has Russia, from which many of its earliest thinkers were drawn – far beyond socialist utopias such as those envisaged by Nahman Syrkin, Ber Borochov, Aaron David Gordon and Berl Katznelson. Today, when young Israelis search for meaning, they are as likely as their diaspora counterparts to find it in a return to the *yeshiva* and to religious tradition. In the process, a profound re-evaluation has taken place in Israel regarding the diaspora and its values. Israelis are far less likely than they were to condemn the *galut*. A survey of Israeli attitudes taken in 1986 showed that most held positive views of diaspora Jewry, and regarded the Jewish people worldwide as their 'extended family'.

What has happened in the move from integration and survival to continuity is that the sharp conflict between Israel and the diaspora has been replaced by at least the possibility of convergence. Both Jewries are beginning to see that *how* we live as Jews may be as important as *where* we live as Jews.

While the sudden rise in assimilation explains this new awareness in the diaspora, it is more difficult to pinpoint its causes in Israel. There are several possible reasons. The first is *yeridah*. An unknown but large number of Israelis now live in the diaspora, in the United States, Britain, South Africa, Australia and elsewhere. No group has disappeared faster from the Jewish map. As has been documented by Moshe Shokeid in his *Children of Circumstances*, secular expatriate Israelis fail to join synagogues or other Jewish organisations and create few if any communal structures of their own. They have no strategy for survival. Since being Jewish means for them living in a Jewish state, once they leave Israel, Jewishness becomes an insoluble dilemma. According to Shokeid, Israelis who have made their home elsewhere maintain a tenuous identity by keeping their names in the Israeli telephone directory and by claiming that their suitcases are packed and that they are merely temporarily detained abroad. Until Israeli-Jewish identity is a matter of *how* as well as *where*, *yordim* will continue to disappear.

The second explanation lies in the new forms which *aliyah* is taking. The early immigrants to Israel were either ideologically motivated or had nowhere else to go. Today, Israel is confronted with two different kinds of immigrant. On the one hand, there are those from Russia who have no knowledge of Judaism, and on the other there are those – most obviously the recent arrivals from Yemen – who are deeply rooted in Jewish tradition. The former have few ties linking them to Israel while the latter are scandalised by its secularity. For the first time, Israel has encountered new arrivals wishing to return, and the more widespread phenomenon of Jews fleeing persecution and making somewhere other than Israel their preferred destination. Hence the concept of *kelitah ruchanit*, 'spiritual absorption', has become part of government policy. Israelis are having to come to terms with the fact that Israel as a destination must have content as well as context.

The third reason, though, is the most central to our argument. Until now, Israel has represented itself to the diaspora as the guarantor of Jewish safety in a hostile world. That idea spoke powerfully to a generation traumatised by the Holocaust but it has diminishing relevance to the next generation who see themselves as safer in London and New York than in Jerusalem, let alone Judea.

It is in this area that recent research findings are very revealing. In 1986, Steven M. Cohen published a survey of American attitudes towards Israel and Israelis, *Ties and Tensions*. In it, he found a lower attachment to Israel among the young than among their parents. Support for Israel is not an inevitable feature of diaspora life. The foremost contemporary historian of Zionism, David Vital, in *The Future of the Jews* (1991), predicts 'a nervous, ever more tenuous, ever less happy association between the Jews of Israel and Jews elsewhere'.

One of Cohen's findings, however, is of the utmost importance. He discovered that *the more Jewishly educated, committed and involved Jews are, the more likely they are to support, fund, visit, identify with and eventually live in Israel*. This marks a development whose significance can hardly be over-emphasised. The either-or has become a both-and. The highly committed section of the Jewish community is more likely *both* to remain Jewish in the diaspora *and* to provide Israel with future support and *aliyah*. The less committed are more likely *both* to marry out in the diaspora *and* to disengage from Israel. Here then is the critical convergence of interests of Israel and the diaspora. Far from negating the diaspora, Israel now needs to strengthen it, even if – *especially* if – it sees itself as the potential home for all Jews.

THE ISRAEL OF CONTINUITY

There is one final step in the argument. Not only does Israel have an *interest* in Jewish continuity worldwide. It is potentially its most powerful *resource*. Once again, though, there must be a paradigm shift. The Israel of survival was Jewry's 'city of refuge', what A.B. Yehoshua called the diaspora's insurance policy. *The Israel of continuity must become Jewry's classroom, the diaspora's ongoing seminar in Jewish identity.* Once, Israel saved Jews. In the future, it will save Judaism.

For nineteen hundred years, the dream of Israel was sufficient to preserve Jewish identity. Today, we have the reality. If Jewish continuity is to be predicated on education, then Israel is Jewry's supreme educational environment. Isaiah's prophecy has been fulfilled in our time: 'From Zion will go forth Torah, and the word of the Lord from Jerusalem.'

Israel is now the only place in which a total Jewish experience is possible. It is the one country where Jews constitute a majority of the population. It is the only context in which they exercise political sovereignty. It is the sole place where Judaism belongs to the public domain, where Hebrew is the language of everyday life and where the Sabbath and the festivals form the rhythm of the calendar. It is the land of our origins, the terrain on which Joshua and David fought and Amos and Isaiah delivered their prophecies. It is the birthplace of Jewish memory and the home of Jewish destiny.

It is impossible to overestimate the impact of Israel on the formation of Jewish identity. Jewish existence, which in today's diaspora may appear random, arbitrary and disconnected, in Israel takes on coherence. There the Bible comes alive against the backdrop of its own landscape and its own language, once again a living tongue. There, too, the concept of the Jewish people becomes vivid in the visible drama of a society gathered together – as Moses said it would be – 'from the ends of the heavens'. Above all, it is in Jerusalem that the mystery of Israel becomes tangible. Here is the old-new heart of the old-new people, the place from which, said Maimonides, the Divine presence never moved.

Jews who spend time in Israel, whether they settle or not, are changed. David Harman, head of the Joint Authority for Jewish Zionist education, reports that among American graduates of Jewish day-schools there is still a twenty-three per cent intermarriage rate. *Among those who have visited Israel the rate drops to four per cent.* The reason, perhaps, is this: Judaism was never the private faith of isolated individuals. Its entire pulse is collective, societal, communal. From the destruction of the second Temple until the end of the eighteenth century, Jews lived in self-governing communities. Exiled from their land they took a fragment of Israel with them. In each locality they had their own language, customs and culture; their collective life. In the modern diaspora, however, Judaism has been confined to the private domain of home, school and synagogue. Israel restores to Jewish life what it has lost elsewhere: a public dimension. Within its borders, Jewishness is *out there* in the street as well as *in here*, in the soul. That is why spending time in Israel is today essential to a full understanding of what it means to be a Jew anywhere in the world.

So we arrive finally at the third policy option for the Jewish future. The diaspora will no longer use its funds to support Israel. Nor will it use them to support itself alone. It will use them to *resource Israel to strengthen the diaspora*, since this is in their joint best interests. It will fund Israel experiences for young Jews. It will make it a goal that every Jewish teenager should spend time in Israel. The Israel-based year of study or service will become normative. The diaspora's teachers will be part-trained in Israel. Its rabbis, youth leaders and outreach workers will study there. There will be more exchanges between Israeli and diaspora teachers and academics. The entire relationship between Israel and the diaspora will shift from dependence to reciprocity.

Future generations will look back in wonder at the strange ideological wars fought between Israel and the diaspora before they reached a symbiotic, mutually supportive relationship. They will be perplexed by Israel's need to negate the diaspora. They will be yet more amazed at the diaspora's tendency to negate itself by devoting its energies to Israel in a way that weakened rather than strengthened its own resources and thus ultimately endangered its long-term support for Israel. It is to be hoped that such self-destructive policies have come to an end. Israel, surely, is our ultimate destination. But the immediate question is less whether Jews are at home in London or Jerusalem than whether they are *at home in their Jewishness*. That is likely to become the leading concern in Israel and the diaspora alike as both turn their attention to continuity.

9
From Jewish Continuity to Jewish Continuity

The analysis is now complete. The time has come to move from reflection to a programme for action. Jews are an intensely practical people. There is an expressive Yiddish monosyllable – the word *Nu* – which brings all theoretical discussion to an end. It means: the analysis is fine, but what then shall we do? The talmudic question, *lemai nafka minei* has the same connotation. It means: what are the practical consequences? We now know that we face a crisis of continuity. What shall we do about it?

Let us remind ourselves why the crisis has occurred. For several generations we have neglected Jewish education. The result is that we know little about Judaism, and our children know even less. They have heard about Israel, but that is a place where they do not live. They have heard about the Holocaust, but that happened sometime else, somewhere else, to people they did not know. They may have experienced antisemitism, but that is not a reason to want their children to be Jewish and thus carry the risk of being exposed to it. They know that Jews like Jewish food, Jewish humour and Jewish friends, but so, too, do many non-Jews. Why then should our children choose not to marry out?

Take 'David', or 'Susan', hypothetical twenty-three-year-olds. They know that when they were young their parents wanted them to go to the best available non-Jewish school. They wanted them to achieve high grades in their secular subjects and go to a good university. Their Jewish education was secondary. They went to *cheder* until *bar* and *bat mitzvah* but if they missed a few weeks here and there, no one minded. As soon as they were old enough to think for themselves, their Jewish education such as it was, ceased. By now they have forgotten what little they learned. What they remember seems childish; *and it is*, because when they learned it they were children. They have no significant memories to make them want to stay Jewish. *Cheder* was boring. The synagogue service was unintelligible. Jewish living is something they do not understand because they never experienced it at home. Now, having been to a non-Jewish school and university, knowing much about non-Jewish culture and little or nothing about their Jewish heritage, they meet a non-Jewish partner, fall in love and want to get married. What argument is there that will persuade them to do otherwise? The short answer is: None.

David and Susan are our children. We neglected their Jewish future for sound and adequate reasons. Our thoughts were elsewhere. We were concerned with social integration. We were worried about Israel. We were alarmed by the threat to Jewish communities in Arab lands and in Eastern Europe. We responded. We succeeded. But in the process, something happened, the full import of which we are only now beginning to grasp. *In saving the Jewish world, we have come perilously close to losing our own children.* In reaching out to help Jews far away, we have forgotten those closest to us. They too needed our help. Now, as the force of Jewish tradition weakens, they need it even more.

THE ONLY ARGUMENT AGAINST INTERMARRIAGE

Times have changed, and we are beginning to sense how suddenly and radically they have changed. We had grown used to a situation in which Jewish identity was passed on through the generations by habit, memory, external events and an inescapable sense that being Jewish is *what we are*. Belatedly we have discovered that for our children, being Jewish is no more than a matter of choice. They know that they can choose otherwise, if not for themselves then for their children. They will choose to be Jewish for one reason only, that knowing the drama of Jewish history, the richness of Jewish life, the grandeur of Jewish ethics and the majesty of Jewish faith, they are *proud to be Jews*.

There is only one cogent argument against intermarriage, and it is this. *To be a Jew is to be a member of the people of the covenant, an heir to one of the world's most ancient, enduring and awe-inspiring faiths. It is to inherit a way of life which has earned the admiration of the world for its love of family, its devotion to education, its philanthropy, its social justice and its infinitely loyal dedication to a unique destiny. It is to know that this way of life, passed on from parents to children since the days of Abraham and Sarah, can only be sustained through the Jewish family; and knowing this, it is to choose to continue it by creating a Jewish home and having Jewish children.* No one who has been touched by Judaism's wings of eternity would willingly break the link between the past and the Jewish future. This and only this will ensure that we have Jewish grandchildren.

How do we achieve this? At the very outset, I knew that this would be the greatest challenge of my Chief Rabbinate, and the greatest single challenge facing today's diaspora as a whole. Despite the fact that the core of the solution is education, the process of acculturation is already too far advanced for this to be our sole response. Most of our children attend, and in the future will continue to attend, non-Jewish schools. There is the question of those who have left school and perhaps have gone to university, or who have already begun their careers. There is the problem of educating parents as well as children, for what will we gain if our children hear one message at school and another conflicting message at home? What about the many social contexts in which young Jews can stay Jewish and which are *not* primarily educational, such as youth clubs, friends, meeting places, organisations and social events? How will any of this help if we do not make our synagogues genuine centres of community, warm, welcoming and all-embracing? A vast global policy is needed, with learning at its heart, but wider than anything normally associated with the word 'education'.

It will be difficult. But it will be possible, *if* we are prepared to change our priorities because times have changed. Two factors might sabotage a solution. The first is despair, which we must resist at all costs. If we believe nothing can be done, then nothing will be done. The Jewish people has never in the past yielded to despair, and now is not the time to begin.

The second factor would be a failure to understand that times *have* changed. Let me candidly admit that I did not go to Jewish schools. Neither did my parents. My generation, and that of our parents and grandparents did not need intensive Jewish education to remind us that we were Jews. But our children belong to the fourth generation. What was enough for us is not enough for them. *In the fourth generation, Judaism is either renewed or it is abandoned: there is no other alternative.*

We are not our parents, and our children are not us. Our parents sought to give us the things they did not have when *they* were children: material comforts, a good secular education, the chance to pursue a profession. They tried to give us the opportunities which they themselves had missed. We in our turn must try to give our children what *we* lacked, namely the chance to experience, live, know and understand our Jewish heritage. That is the challenge.

A NEW FRAMEWORK

It is a vast challenge, complex and profound. It will call for a response at many levels of our Jewish life, as individuals, members of families and participants in congregations. But my concern here is with only one dimension, namely our *collective* response as Anglo-Jewry.

We need a new community-wide organisation. The reason is simple. There are many religious and educational bodies in Anglo-Jewry and many youth groups and outreach programmes. Each is valuable and each has a vital role to play. But there is nothing that puts them together into a coherent strategy. The result is fragmentation and creative chaos – creative, but chaos none the less.

A single body is needed *to promote, plan and resource all those many activities in our community which create Jewish continuity.* Its task will be *to intensify Jewish life in such a way as to create future generations of Jews who are proud, knowledgeable and committed as Jews.* To do so it will have to aim at nothing less than a complete transformation of Anglo-Jewish attitudes, so that continuity moves from last to first place on our communal agenda. The new organisation will have to become the third arm of Anglo-Jewry, alongside Israel and welfare. The clearest test of its success or failure will be whether in five years' time education is still languishing at the bottom of our list of communal charities or whether it has made its claim to at least equal status with the other two causes. If we succeed, Anglo-Jewry will have a future. If we fail, its future is altogether in doubt.

To my knowledge, no other diaspora community has ever attempted a project on this scale. Each has its educational bodies. But none has a global, community-wide strategy for continuity. In the main, schools, synagogues, youth groups, adult education and outreach projects operate independently of one another. The result is less like a strategy, more like a dodgem-car track, with many vehicles moving in random directions, more often colliding than cohering. This is wasteful of energies and resources and cannot be the best way to proceed. If Anglo-Jewry is to be the first diaspora community to bring order out of chaos, so be it. There is no alternative if we are to solve the greatest problem facing Jewry outside of Israel, and therefore we must begin.

WHO CONTINUES?

To do so I had first to answer three questions. The first and most fundamental was whom would the new organisation be aimed at? At committed Jewry, or at all Jews?

There is one widely held view which I call Jewish Darwinism. It holds that throughout the generations, only the fittest Jews survive. At all times, and especially in an open society, Jews leave the fold. They opt out, marry out and disappear. Only the most dedicated remain.

On this reading, it is futile to speak of continuity as a programme for all Jews. Instead, one should concentrate on the committed. They are Jewry's survivalists. Only they will have Jewish grandchildren. Their schools, *yeshivot* and houses of study will compensate for Jewish ignorance elsewhere; their large families will make up for Jews lost elsewhere. In an age in which eighty per cent of young Jews see nothing wrong in intermarriage, there is no point in even talking to eighty per cent of young Jews, let alone wasting resources on them. Rather, we should focus exclusively on the twenty per cent who will survive.

Though this position has many adherents, I reject it absolutely. I have explained my reasons, at length, in my books *Arguments for the Sake of Heaven* and *One People?* I reject it because it is not the way of Abraham or Moses, who wrestled with wayward generations and refused to write them off. I reject it because it is not the way of the great Jewish leaders of our time, the late Rabbis Kook and Soloveitchik, and the present Lubavitcher Rebbe, Rabbi Menachem Mendel Schneersohn.

I reject it because it mistakes fact for principle, confusing what may happen if we do nothing with what we have allowed to happen. I reject it because after the Holocaust in which we lost eighty per cent of European Jewry, we cannot stand idly by while a spiritual holocaust takes its toll of eighty per cent of the Jews who remain. I reject it because as a human being and as a believing Jew I cannot live at ease with the knowledge that twenty per cent of my people will survive while I and they failed to extend a hand to the eighty per cent whose Jewish future is at risk.

I reject it, above all, because Jewish destiny is a collective destiny, defined by a covenant which links all Jews in a bond of shared responsibility. Every Jew is a fragment of the *Shekhinah*, the Divine presence which dwells in the heart of Jews wherever and whatever they are. When the Israelites made the Golden Calf, God proposed to destroy the people there and then and to begin afresh with Moses. Moses replied: 'Please forgive their sin – but if not, then blot me out of the book You have written.' This is and must be the Jewish response: *collective*, not *selective* survival.

The new organisation, then, will be aimed at *all* Jews in the unshakable belief that every Jew is precious.

FROM EDUCATION TO CONTINUITY

The second question is to define the nature of the challenge, and thus provide the new organisation with a clear identity and purpose, a 'mission statement'. It is here that we made a fundamental choice: we would speak not about Jewish *education* but about Jewish *continuity*.

In the past, Jewish education was understood as the acquisition of knowledge, understanding and skills. Jewish *identity* was taken for granted. Today, it can no longer be taken for granted. It has to be created. I believe that the main vehicle for creating Jewish identity in the diaspora is education. But there is a difference between education as an end in itself and as a means for sustaining Jewish identity across the generations.

Education was always important to Jews. Our generation is unique in that *it is the first in 2,500 years of history in which a majority of young Jews in the diaspora is deciding not to marry another Jew, create a Jewish home and have Jewish children*. This what lends our project its particular urgency and direction.

Not all education creates continuity, and not everything that creates continuity is education. On the one hand, there are programmes of Jewish study which aim at detachment rather than commitment and which can be participated in equally by non-Jews and Jews. These are important and valuable but they fall outside the scope of this project. On the other, there are programmes which are not explicitly educational but which may be highly effective in creating Jewish involvement, such as youth centres, community service programmes, Israel visits and singles groups. These would fall within our brief. In general, however, there can be no sustainable and transmissible Jewish identity without learning and knowledge. So 'education' and 'continuity' substantially overlap but they are not identical.

I believe that in framing matters in this way we are reverting to a more traditional Jewish concept of education. The Talmud asks which is greater, *talmud* or *maaseh*, Jewish learning or Jewish living? It answers: Jewish learning is greater because it *leads* to Jewish living. Education, then, is not an end in itself but a path to something else. Jewishly, learning is tested not by passing exams but by *how I live*. If I become a great scholar but I do not live Jewishly, then my education has been an academic success but a Jewish failure. The fundamental value is Jewish living.

When the Torah speaks about education it does so in a striking and unusual way. It does not speak – as do the great Greek thinkers, Plato and Aristotle – of academies, schools, classrooms, pupils, the search for knowledge and the quest for truth. It speaks of parents and children and handing on the tradition from one generation to the next. Abraham is chosen – 'so that he will instruct his children and his household after him to keep the way of the Lord, doing what is right and just'. The *Shema* commands us: 'Teach these things diligently to your children, speaking of them when you sit at home and when you journey on the way, when you lie down and when you rise up.' The *seder* service on Pesach – Judaism's most intense and revolutionary educational experience – involves teaching a child to see himself or herself as part of a people and its memories, and it is achieved not by teachers in class-rooms but by parents around the family table. Jewish education is not about the abstract contemplation of truth. It is about introducing the next generation to the covenant which they inherit from their parents and their parents' parents through a family line which stretches back to Sinai. Jewish education is about Jewish continuity.

So we arrived at a name and a mission statement for the organisation. It will be called *Jewish Continuity*, and its aim will be *to secure the future of Anglo-Jewry by creating a vibrant community of proud, knowledgeable and committed Jews.*

FROM FRAGMENTATION TO STRATEGY

The third question is no less fundamental. The past twenty-five years have witnessed a considerable investment by diaspora communities in Jewish education. Jewish day-schools have been built. In America, though to a much lesser extent in Britain, there has been a proliferation of Jewish Studies programmes at universities. Yet assimilation, out-marriage and disengagement have proceeded apace. *If education is the answer why is there still a problem?*

The short answer is this: there has been education but not an educational strategy, still less a considered programme for continuity. In the process, two things have been overlooked. One is *coverage*, the other is *reinforcement*.

The growth of Jewish day-schools since the end of the Second World War has been one of the great achievements of diaspora Jewry in modern times. However, while full-time Jewish education has flourished, the part-time system – *cheder*, Hebrew Classes or supplementary schooling – has declined. Recent studies in Britain and America have concluded that the part-time system is weak and growing weaker, with under-qualified teachers, bored and listless children and indifferent parents. The result is a polarisation of the Jewish educational experience for the young. For some – still a minority – their education is becoming more intensive. For others, it is becoming less substantial year by year.

Ironically, while the numbers attending Jewish day-schools have grown, so too have the numbers receiving little or no Jewish education. It therefore comes as no surprise that while Jewish schools have multiplied, so too has the intermarriage rate. The Jewish community is beginning to divide, less between Orthodoxy and others or between religious and secular, but between those who *know* and those who do not. And because participation in the Jewish community requires a certain minimum of knowledge, those who lack that knowledge will inevitably feel alienated: spectators at an event they do not understand.

A strategy for continuity would therefore examine *coverage*. It would ask what is happening to *all* Jews, not just those at Jewish schools. Equally important, it would explore the dynamics of *reinforcement*.

It was once thought that Jewish day-schools, in and by themselves, would solve the problem of Jewish continuity. Since education was good, more education must be better, and the Jewish day-school offered the most intensive form of education available outside the *yeshiva*. This theory neglected the fact that the school is only one influence on the child. Friends and peer-groups, the wider society (in particular, the media), and above all, parents and home all affect a child's development. Where these other influences conflict with the school, the child experiences 'cognitive dissonance', a tension between different sets of messages. Schools succeed when they are supported by the rest of the child's experience of the world. When they are unsupported they fail.

Schools work when they are part of a global strategy of identity formation and reinforcement. Often, we lack such a strategy. To take a simple example: in London several Jewish primary schools achieved fine results in teaching their pupils to speak *Ivrit*, only to find that this programme was not carried through in the curriculum of the Jewish secondary schools. Within months the children had forgotten what they had been so assiduously taught.

There are communities throughout Britain which have excellent Jewish primary schools, but which lack Jewish secondary schools. Indeed, some communities do not even have a *policy* for teenagers. Some children join Jewish youth groups, but many do not. Another gap: in most universities there are Jewish student societies and Hillel Houses. There are Jewish university chaplains. But there is little or no provision for young Jews *leaving* university. They are not yet married and are just setting out on a career. If they enter a synagogue or join a Jewish organisation, they will find few of their contemporaries there. There are too few places where they can mix, meet and feel that they belong. Teenage and post-university are critical stages of identity formation. The excellent work done by primary schools and university chaplains can go to waste simply because there is no follow-through, no global planning.

A coherent strategy for continuity would look at what happens to children outside the classroom as well as within, and at what happens when one life-phase ends and another begins. It would examine the Jewish home, the peer-group, the synagogue and other institutional expressions of Jewish life and strive to forge links between them. It would look at critical moments of transition. It would be based on careful research, monitoring and evaluation. It would discover what works and what does not; which Jewish experiences are positive and which negative; where the community loses Jews and where it can hope to attract them.

We realised that we would have to revolutionise the way we *think* about continuity. Until now we have thought about *institutions* – schools, synagogues and so on – and sought excellence from them. That is right and proper, but it is the wrong place to begin. Instead, we must think about *people*. People are exposed to many influences over a lifetime, and at times make decisions that will affect the rest of their lives. Schools, synagogues, youth groups and student societies are all part of this larger framework and we must view them from that perspective. What makes people proud to be Jews? What makes them involved as Jews? What makes them want to have Jewish grandchildren? These are the questions we will continually have to ask. So Jewish Continuity will have a global, integrated and people-based strategy.

Many other decisions needed to be made about organisational style and objectives, and I have set these out in an appendix. But the overall aims of Jewish Continuity are clear. It will be a community-wide organisation encompassing all activities which promote Jewish continuity across the generations. It will seek to secure the future of Anglo-Jewry by creating a vibrant community of proud, knowledgeable and committed Jews. It is built upon the principles that every Jew is precious, that Jewish life has a distinctive spiritual and ethical content, and that Jewish identity can only be sustained in the long run by Jewish learning, experiencing and doing.

Through the structures it creates, the tasks it undertakes and the funds it raises, Jewish Continuity will promote the importance of continuity until it becomes the first item on the Anglo-Jewish agenda. It will develop a strategy for continuity, informed by research, monitoring and evaluation. It will create an informed and energetic lay leadership dedicated to the task. It will seek to increase funding for continuity-creating projects, including Jewish day-schools, Jewish enrichment at non-Jewish schools, youth groups, adult, informal and family education, student societies, university chaplaincy, outreach activities, residential retreats and Israel experiences. It will allocate funds in such a way as to ensure a rational distribution of resources, minimising waste and duplication and encouraging excellence, creativity, coverage, integration and reinforcement. It will focus on the 'people' dimension of continuity, the recruitment and training of teachers, youth leaders, adult educators and outreach workers. It will create a central and nationally available pool of resources and specialised expertise. By these means it will strive to raise levels of knowledge of and participation in Jewish life.

TODAY'S QUESTION

It is less than a year since the words 'Jewish Continuity' first coalesced in my mind as an idea, a problem and the glimmerings of a solution. Since then my office has engaged in consultation with rabbis, educators, youth leaders, outreach workers, academics, lay leaders and communal representatives. We have drafted and redrafted proposals and subjected them to the detailed scrutiny of the world's leading Jewish educational planners at a special consultation in Jerusalem. We have recruited impressive groups of lay leaders, supporters and advisers, and begun to put in place our professional team and initial projects. We have had the benefit of many exceptional individuals. We are now ready to begin.

Throughout this whole process one thing has become clear: Jewish Continuity is an idea whose time has come. We are about to enter the third great era of modern Jewry. Almost everyone we have spoken to agrees that the single most burning question in today's diaspora is: will we have Jewish grandchildren? If we act now to make continuity our first priority, we will.

There are deep questions which I have not attempted to answer here, and they are crucial to the project of Jewish continuity. What does it mean to be Jewish today? Are there modes of Jewish 'belonging' for those alienated from Judaism's religious faith and way of life? Is Jewish education effective, or does some of it fail to touch those to whom it is addressed? And most simply and searchingly: why *be* Jewish in an age when disaffiliation is possible?

I recognise the force of these questions, and I hope to address them elsewhere. We must begin somewhere, however. I have chosen to begin, intellectually and organisationally, with the question: what can we do as a community? The attrition which today threatens the future of the diaspora is not inevitable. It is the result of communal decisions and ways of thinking which may have been justifiable in the past but are so no longer. Jewish Continuity is not of itself a total solution to the formation and transmission of a positive Jewish identity. It is an attempt to create the necessary framework. By focusing our minds, energies and resources on continuity, we will make it the arena within which solutions will be tested and put into practice.

We have, I believe, no alternative if we are to keep faith with the Jewish past and the Jewish future. As we look back on this extraordinary century – the century in which *Yom ha-Shoah, Yom ha-Atzma'ut* and *Yom Yerushalayim* were added to the Jewish calendar – we have cause to wonder and to give thanks. I cannot fathom the mysteries of the Holocaust. But I know this, that after one of the greatest tragedies in human history, the Jewish people has emerged from the valley of the shadow of death and found independence and sovereignty in the land of its birth, and freedom and affluence in most countries of the diaspora. But one question reverberates throughout the Jewish world today. *What will God have given us if we gain all else and lose our own children?* Jewish Continuity begins with that question. We will not forgive ourselves nor will posterity forgive us if we fail. With the help of God, we will succeed.

10
Epilogue

There is a mystery at the heart of Jewish existence, and it is written into the first syllables of our recorded time.

The first words of God to Abraham were: 'Go out from your land, your birthplace, and your father's house to the land which I will show you. And I will make you a great nation...'

Then Abraham receives another promise: 'I will make your children like the dust of the earth, so that if anyone could count the dust of the earth, then could your offspring be counted.'

There is yet another promise: 'God took him outside and said, "Look up at the heavens and count the stars – if indeed you can count them." Then He said to him, "So shall your children be."'

Three escalating promises: Abraham would be the father of a great nation; he would be the father of as many children as the dust of the earth; he would be the father of as many children as the stars in heaven.

What, though, was the reality? Early on in the story, after his brief stay in Egypt, we read that Abraham was 'very wealthy in livestock and in silver and gold'. He had everything except one thing: a child. Then God appears to Abraham and says, 'Do not be afraid. I am your shield. Your reward will be very great.' Until this point, Abraham has been silent. Now, something within him breaks and he asks: 'O Lord God, what will You give me if I remain childless?' *The first recorded words of man to God in the history of the covenant are a plea for there to be future generations.* The first Jew feared he would be the last.

Then God gave Abraham a child, born to Sarah's handmaid Hagar. His name was Ishmael which means 'God will hear'. Evidently, Abraham believed that God had answered his prayer and given him a son. But in the very next chapter we learn that Ishmael was not destined to be a child of the covenant. He would be blessed. He would be fruitful. He would be the father of twelve princes. He would become a great nation. But he was not the child of Jewish destiny, and Abraham would one day have to part company with him.

This fact pains Abraham deeply. Twice, he registers his grief.

When he first discovers his son's fate, he pleads: 'If only Ishmael might live under Your blessing.' Later, when Sarah drives Ishmael away, we read that 'This troubled Abraham very much because it involved his son.' None the less, God confirms Sarah's decision. Abraham must lose his son.

Now, another son is promised. His name will be Isaac and he will be born to Sarah. This is a biological impossibility. Sarah is already ninety and, as the Bible tells us, post-menopausal. Neither Abraham nor Sarah can believe it. Abraham 'fell on his face and laughed. He said to himself: can a hundred-year-old man have children? Can Sarah, who is ninety, give birth?' Sarah 'laughed to herself, saying: Now that I am worn out and my husband is old, shall I have this pleasure?' The sages found this disbelief difficult to comprehend, and in the case of Abraham they softened it. The Targum, the Aramaic translation of the Bible, turns Abraham's laughter into celebration, but the plain sense of the verse is inescapable. Abraham laughed with incredulity.

Against natural possibility, Isaac is born. Sarah says: 'God has given me laughter.' The strange story seems to have reached a happy ending. It has taken time and much waiting and long-deferred hopes. A son has arrived at the last moment, or, as far as Sarah's fertility is concerned, after the last moment. Throughout the narrative we have sensed in countless ways the strain which Abraham and Sarah have undergone. Their characters are sharply drawn and the portrayal remains vivid to this day. Finally, in Sarah's laughter, we feel the tension ebb away. The couple relax. They have a child at last. They are fulfilled.

And then in the next chapter we read the words that in all the intervening years have not lost their power to shock:

After these events, God tested Abraham. He said to him, 'Abraham!' He replied, 'Here I am.' Then God said, 'Take your son, your only son, the one whom you love – Isaac – and go to the region of Moriah. Sacrifice him there as a burnt offering on one of the mountains that I will show you.

Abraham gathers his son, travels for three days, climbs the mountain, prepares the wood, ties his son, takes the knife and raises his hand. Then a voice is heard from heaven: 'Do not lay a hand on the boy.' The trial is over. Isaac lives.

The enigma is almost overpowering. On the one hand there were the promises: a great nation, as many children as the dust, as many children as the stars. But set against them was the long drawn-out agony.

The years of childlessness. Then the child who was sent away. Then the child who could not be born, but was. Then the decree of death against this one child, countermanded at the last moment. We cannot read this strange, tantalising sequence of events without asking: why?

PRECIOUSNESS AND LOSS

The story of Jewish continuity is a mystery. It is so today, as the century of the Holocaust and the rebirth of Israel draws to a close. It was so from the beginning, from the days of Abraham and Sarah.

According to the Bible, if nature had taken its course, Sarah would not have had a child and there would have been no Jewish people. If Abraham had had his way and been content with Ishmael, there would have been no Jewish people. If Isaac had been born but the word from heaven had been delayed, telling Abraham to stay his hand, Isaac would have died and there would have been no Jewish people. On such slender avoidance of the probable does Jewish continuity rest.

Nor does the evidence derive from the Torah alone. I began this book with the first two recorded references to Israel outside the Bible. According to Merneptah in the thirteenth century BCE, Israel had been destroyed. According to Mesha, king of Moab, Israel had been destroyed. Such was the verdict of Israel's enemies from Pharaoh to Haman to Hitler. Few, if any, other peoples have been the subject of so many decrees of genocide. Few could have read their own obituary more often. The binding of Isaac has been rehearsed not once but many times in our history. As a people, we are no strangers to the angel of death. But the Jewish people lives.

As we search these ancient texts, perhaps we begin to understand. It is as if a certain message was woven into our being from the very outset. To move from one generation of Jews to the next requires a miracle: a series of miracles. At every stage in the transition from Abraham and Sarah to Isaac, continuity seems to be impossible. Nature is against it. Prediction rules otherwise. At times, even Heaven itself seems to conspire against it. We are Jews today by virtue of miracles.

Imagine trying to trace your family tree back beyond *booba* and *zeida* to their grandparents, and theirs. In the strange, tortuous, tangled chain which links Abraham and Sarah with us, is a succession of miracles which confound belief. Somehow, our ancestors survived the destructions and the exiles, the Crusades and the Blood Libels, the forced conversions and the Inquisitions, the persecutions and the pogroms; survived, by accident or destiny, the Final Solution and the gas chambers. Somehow, our parents and their parents and all the generations before them lived through the hopelessness and despair, the wanderings and sufferings, and against prediction and logic, brought new generations of Jewish children into the world. There has been nothing like it in the history of humanity. Can we, dare we, be the last generation?

We cherish what we most risk losing. Might it be that our history as a nation began with slavery in Egypt so that we would always know what it felt like to be slaves and thus become the people driven by a passion for freedom? Might it be that we were condemned to live most of our history in exile so that love of the land – above all, Jerusalem, home of the Divine presence – should be engraved upon our hearts? Might it be that we were forced so often to walk through the valley of the shadow of death in order to learn Judaism's most fundamental ethical imperative: the unconditional sanctity of life. Might it be that, like Jonah and the gourd, we were taught to cherish what must be cherished by having it taken away from us?

With these questions we begin to fathom the mystery of Abraham and Sarah and of the next generation. The promises, the delay, the hope, the despair, the torments, the trials, the disappointed expectations could have no other effect than to create, at the very beginning of Jewish time, a focus bordering on an obsession with Jewish children. No other people has cared more for its children, invested more energy in them and shaped the whole of its religious life in order to hand on to them what it finds precious. *Abraham and Sarah had a child because they so nearly did not have a child.* Other cultures take children for granted. Judaism has never taken its children for granted, because Jews have known what it is like to be an Abraham or Sarah. So often were we in danger of losing our chidren, through persecution or assimilation, that they became our driving concern. We risked losing them. Therefore we cherished them.

GIVING TO THE FUTURE AND TO THE PAST

Today, we are losing our children. I have tried to explain why. For three generations we were preoccupied with other pressing, important concerns which touched on the very existence of the Jew in the modern world. We could be forgiven for neglecting the Jewishness of our children. There were other matters to attend to first. There was integration. There was survival. Not since the days of the destruction of the second Temple nineteen centuries ago has the Jewish people faced such dislocation, such collective trauma.

That crisis has now passed. Today we face a new situation in our 4,000-year history: the challenge of creating a Jewish life in conditions of freedom and equality in the diaspora and sovereignty in our own land, the land of Israel. That was always the ultimate challenge, and it reverberates throughout the lines of Jewish destiny. We survived slavery. Can we survive freedom? We survived suffering. Can we survive security? We survived exile. Can we survive homecoming?

We will do none of these things unless, at long last, we put our children and their Jewish needs first. The Bible provides us with the key to the ultimate question which has puzzled Jew and non-Jew alike. Why Abraham? Why Israel? Why the Jewish people? Abraham, says the Torah, was chosen 'so that he will direct his children and his household after him to keep the way of the Lord by doing what is right and just'. Abraham was chosen not for himself but for his children and for what he would create in them: a way of life that they would value and continue and pass on. They would be a link in a chain of eternity.

Not all of us can have children. But each of us can do something to ensure the continuity of the Jewish people. We can make it possible for every Jewish child to experience, learn about and live the heritage which earned the admiration, and changed the civilisation, of the world. We need now to relearn the oldest Jewish instinct of all: that precious values should live on through us into the next generation.

Let us not treat the future lightly. When God promised Abraham that his reward would be very great, he replied: 'O Lord God, what will you give me if I remain childless?' That is the question eternity asks of us. What meaning will our lives and the lives of our ancestors have if they are not lent immortality by our continuity, by our bringing it about that we have Jewish grandchildren? If we would only remember the many miracles it took to bring us to this hour, we would willingly do our duty to ensure that the next generation stays Jewish, and the generation after that. Jewish continuity is the greatest gift we can bring to the future and the past.

Appendix

THE STRUCTURE OF CONTINUITY

There is no single way of securing Jewish continuity. That fact lies at the heart of our organisation. Let us think of our own Jewish life and ask what has contributed to its Jewishness. There were the formal experiences of the synagogue and Jewish instruction. There were informal encounters that were sometimes no less potent: friends, youth groups, student societies or a visit to Israel. There may have been negative moments, experiences of antisemitism, which made us suddenly conscious of who we are. Above all, there was the formative influence of childhood and of growing up in a Jewish home. Each of these factors plays its part in shaping how we see ourselves as Jews and contributes to those ultimate decisions which determine whether or not we will hand on a Jewish identity to the next generation.

Can there be, therefore, an overall strategy for continuity and an organisation capable of implementing it? The answer is yes. It involves promoting those activities which lead to positive, knowledgeable and transmissible Jewish identity. Which activities are effective and which are not can be tested and evaluated by research. Clarity of vision must be accompanied by flexibility of method and an understanding of the multi-faceted nature of Jewish experience. Jonathan Woocher put it best when he wrote:

> What should we actually do to promote Jewish continuity? In principle we should do everything. Our best strategy would be to build a massive array of opportunities for Jews to be Jewish ... We know that Jewishnessness is a cumulative experience. The more one is involved in one aspect of being Jewish the more likely one will be involved in others ... The key is not to focus on any one experience, to seek the one decisive moment or programme, but to lay the broad pavement along which the Jewish journey can proceed.

Hence it is imperative for there to be an organisational framework spanning the entire range of Jewish activity. The strength of Jewish life is to be found at the grass roots: in individual communities, synagogues, schools and pioneering initiatives. These form our multiple centres of Jewish excellence. Yet, unless there are connections between them, they are capable of subverting one another.

Unless parents grow Jewishly along with their children, the home can frustrate the efforts of the school. Unless synagogues are open, warm and welcoming, they can sabotage the best endeavours of outreach programmes. Unless a community pays attentions to the needs of Jews between leaving school and getting married, the arduous process of Jewish education can come to grief as children emerge into adulthood and find themselves unsupported at a decisive period of transition.

So we must create an organisation that will strengthen individual institutions while at the same time shaping and implementing an all-embracing strategy. The key decisions which we have taken are these:

Jewish Continuity should be a *lean* and *enabling* organisation. It will empower the people and organisations in the field. It will not engage directly in education and outreach. It will resource those who are. It will give them the help they need to do their work better.

Jewish Continuity will *implement strategy by 'steering, not rowing'*. It will shape policy by the decisions it takes to fund this project rather than that one. It will make its funding conditional on objectives, whether these concern quality control, or networking, or success in reaching target populations. Where it identifies a gap in communal provision, it will contract it out to organisations with the most appropriate record of achievement. It will encourage educators, rabbis, youth workers, student leaders and outreach practitioners to engage in problem solving, lateral thinking, integration and innovation. It will work through, not over the heads of, local organisations.

Jewish Continuity will be a *national, community-wide, overarching body* involving schools, synagogues, youth groups, student societies, university chaplaincy, informal, family and adult education. It will attempt to enlist Israel and welfare organisations as well. It will be broadly based, so that every Jewish community in Britain will have its own Jewish Continuity committee, its local leaders and its own development plan.

Jewish Continuity will be a *task-oriented* organisation. Its aim is not to achieve a consensus on what constitutes Jewish identity, literacy or commitment. No such consensus is currently available. The Jewish community is fragmented. It contains a host of institutions whose visions and interests conflict. Were we to aim for agreement on matters which have divided Jews for the past two centuries, we would invite a decade of sterile debate. Instead, Jewish Continuity will recognise the diversity of ways in which Jews arrive at Jewish commitment. It will encourage those activities which make a positive difference to Jewish lives, and to the Judaic strength of the next generation. It will set a

Appendix: The Structure of Continuity

priority on creativity, excellence and innovation rather than on a common-denominator approach to Jewish life.

What then are our objectives?

1. Vision

The first task of Jewish Continuity is to create a vision and a sense of urgency. The future of Anglo-Jewry, indeed of the diaspora as a whole, is at risk. I have tried to show why it is at risk. For generations we have concentrated on social integration and physical survival. In the process, we have neglected the continuity of Jewish identity. Until recently we could take it for granted. We can do so no longer.

We will have succeeded if, and only if, Anglo-Jewry places identity-formation at the top of its communal agenda. For this to happen, there must be more than a sense of crisis. There must be genuine conviction that Jewishness and Judaism matter, that they are precious, and that they must be handed on to the next generation.

I have concentrated in this book on the crisis. I have said less – and much more needs to be said – about the conviction. As Jacob Neusner puts it, 'When we know *why* we want to survive, what difference it makes for us to continue as a distinctive group, we shall have no problem finding out *how*.'

Continuity depends on confidence, which depends in turn on content. For centuries Jews passed on their faith and way of life to their children, not because they had no alternative, nor because of unquestioning loyalty to the past, but because they believed in Judaism's dedication to the family, the community, education, philanthropy, social justice and individual righteousness. They believed that being Jewish was the best way for a Jew to be a human being.

A century of trauma, antisemitism and anti-Zionism has left its mark on the Jewish soul. It has left us defensive and insecure. But we must eventually awake from the nightmare and recover our self-respect. If not, we will continue to be ambivalent about our Jewishness and we will convey mixed messages to our children.

Jewish Continuity rests on a vision which it must communicate: that to be a Jew is to be an heir to one of the greatest traditions of faith, morality, community and individual living the world has ever known.

2. Leadership

Continuity needs 'champions', individuals who will turn vision into reality. Jewish Continuity will recruit lay leaders and undertake not merely to energise them but also to educate them in what Anglo-Jewry does and what it might do – focusing on models of best practice both here and abroad. It will concentrate on new leadership, young leadership and recruiting excellence. It will also aim to match leaders to tasks, and to encourage movement in communal leadership so that people are regularly faced with fresh challenges, and challenges are met by new faces.

3. Resources
Jewish Continuity will aim to generate resources for education and outreach in all its forms. Because it will aim to secure not only funds but also commitment and involvement, it will be judged not only by the sums it raises but by the number of donors it secures.

It will raise funds for three purposes. First, it will resource Jewish Continuity itself, with the proviso that it must remain a lean, enabling organisation with the minimum budget necessary to achieve its ends. The principles are that it will not do anything done by any other organisation, that it will not engage in education at the point of delivery but instead work through organisations in the field, that it will not do anything that could be done effectively at the local level, and that it will employ a minimum of paid staff.

Second and more importantly, it will support existing bodies through project-based funding, and direct this support in such a way as to influence the development of education in line with its overall strategy. Third, it will help existing bodies to fundraise for themselves. One way in which it will do so will be by creating a national campaign in which money is returned directly to the localities where, and the bodies for whom, it was raised.

4. A Communal Strategy
Jewish Continuity will develop a community-wide strategy for Jewish learning, experiencing and doing in all forms and contexts and for all ages and groups. It will implement this strategy by the way it allocates funds and resources.

Within the context of an overall, long-term vision, it will develop a five-year plan, to be reviewed annually. It will develop broad criteria of success, together with quantifiable targets for specific tasks. It will develop structures of accountability for the achievement of its targets. At its core will be the perception best expressed by Jonathan Woocher: 'The new Jewish mosaic we envision will have to be built one tile at a

Appendix: The Structure of Continuity

time. The challenge is to remember the grand design as we put each piece into place.'

5. *An integrated strategy*
The greatest weakness of Jewish education throughout the diaspora is its fragmentation. Jewish Continuity will address this problem directly. As an overarching, enabling body it will not own schools or programmes, but it will help to resource them in a structured way, so as to advance an overall plan. Where cooperation or rationalisation are necessary, these will be promoted and made a condition of support. In cases where gaps exist, Jewish Continuity will ensure that they are filled by the organisations with the most appropriate available skills.

6. *A research-based strategy*
The Jewish community has finite resources but potentially infinite demands. Too often in the past, spending decisions have been made on the basis of institutional interests, special pleading, even personal whim. Prestige projects of limited impact have sometimes gained at the expense of essential services, such as teacher training and curriculum development. Jewish Continuity will commission research and independent evaluation so that the effectiveness of different forms and institutions can be monitored and assessed.

7. *Promoting people*
Creating continuity depends almost entirely on people. A school or an adult education programme can be housed in poor buildings, but they can transform the lives of those they touch. Identity and commitment are shaped not by buildings but by relationships between people. While not excluding capital projects from its remit, Jewish Continuity will concentrate on the 'people dimension' of education.

Jewish Continuity will therefore develop a strategy for recruiting and training educators, pre- and in-service. It will aim to raise standards not only of teachers in schools but also of youth and community workers, outreach workers and adult educators. In doing so, it will work in conjunction with teachers, head-teachers and governors so that they share ownership in and responsibility for the process. It will enlist the best available expertise, not only within Anglo-Jewry, but drawing also on the resources of secular institutions in Britain and Jewish institutions elsewhere, especially in Israel.

8. Making connections

Jewish Continuity takes as a well-documented premise that moments of Jewish learning, experiencing and living are most effective when they are reinforced. It will therefore encourage a holistic approach to continuity, bringing together schools, youth groups, the synagogue, informal, family and adult education, Israel experiences and forms of community service. It will do this in a variety of ways: through *lead communities* which become pilot projects for an integrated strategy in a particular locality, *networking* of layleaders and professionals, and *community-wide projects* which involve bringing different agencies, leaders and professionals together.

9. A bias towards outreach and innovation

Jewish Continuity cannot, by itself, meet all the needs of the Anglo-Jewish future, nor would it be desirable for it to do so. It must aim to empower and facilitate the localities and organisations directly involved. Even so, it must establish priorities. Therefore, though it will be supportive of all ventures that create continuity, it will embody a bias towards those institutions and projects which most affect Jews whose involvement in Jewish life is marginal.

It will, as part of its strategy, identify constituencies for which little or nothing exists in the form of contexts for learning about or experiencing Jewish life or forming Jewish relationships. It will also focus on key moments of affiliation and disaffiliation, such as leaving home for university or work, leaving university, getting married, having children and arranging for their education.

Once it has identified gaps in communal provision, Jewish Continuity will encourage and resource individuals or organisations to develop creative projects that speak to the needs of such groups or moments. It will work through those closest to the problem, and will facilitate contact between those who know the constituency and those who have the requisite skills. In short, Jewish Continuity will have a bias towards outreach and innovation.

10. A learning community

At the core of Jewish Continuity is the realisation that Jewish identity in the diaspora is not something that happens of its own accord. It must be learned and lived, acted out and constantly reinforced. In this process, much depends on our choices as individuals. Much, too, depends on our decisions as a community. Does Anglo-Jewry care about itself as much as it cares about communities elsewhere? Does it care about its junior as well as its senior citizens? Does it care about its future as much as about its past? Is continuity fully equal, in our communal priorities, to Israel and welfare?

We must aim at a community in which, in Alvin Schiff's words, 'Jewish youth are exposed to and involved in a confluence of cognitive-affective Jewish experiences in a Jewish school (preferably elementary and secondary day school), synagogue, youth group, summer camp and home (via Jewish family education, where appropriate). And all this capped by an Israel experience during the teen years, especially a post-high school year of study in Israel.' We must take collective delight in learning and growing as Jews.

Jewish Continuity is not, in itself, a complete answer to the complex problem of safeguarding the Jewish future. Nevertheless, it will provide Anglo-Jewry with a disciplined structure from within which answers will emerge. Its task is to provide vision, leadership, strategy, resources and research. It is not too much to say that on its success the future of Anglo-Jewry depends.

Bibliography

ACKERMAN, WALTER I., *The Structure of Jewish Education*, Commission on Jewish Education in North America, 1990.
ALDERMAN, GEOFFREY, *Modern British Jewry*, Clarendon Press, Oxford, 1992.
AVIAD, JANET (ed.), *Studies in Jewish Education*, Vol.3, Magnes Press, Jerusalem, 1988.
BAYME, STEVEN, 'Ensuring Jewish Continuity', *Journal of Jewish Community Service*, Vol.68 No.4 (Summer 1992), pp.335–41.
BROOK, STEPHEN, *The Club: The Jews of Modern Britain*, Constable, London, 1989.
CHAZAN, BARRY (ed.), *Studies in Jewish Education*, Vol.1, Magnes Press, Jerusalem, 1983.
COHEN, STEVEN M., *American Modernity and Jewish Identity*, Tavistock, London, 1983.
—— *American Assimilation or Jewish Revival?*, Indiana University Press, Bloomington, 1988.
—— 'Ties and Tensions: The 1986 Survey of American Jewish Attitudes toward Israel and Israelis', The American Jewish Committee, 1987.
COHEN, STEVEN M., and FEIN, LEONARD J., 'From Integration to Survival: American Jewish Anxieties in Transition', *Annals of the American Academy of Political and Social Science*, July 1985, pp.75–88.
COMMISSION ON JEWISH EDUCATION IN NORTH AMERICA, *A Time to Act*, University Press of America, Lanham, 1991.
COOPER, HOWARD and MORRISON, PAUL, *A Sense of Belonging: Dilemmas of British Jewish Identity*, Weidenfeld & Nicolson, London, 1991.
CUDDIHY, JOHN MURRAY, *The Ordeal of Civility: Freud, Marx, Levi-Strauss and the Jewish Struggle with Modernity*, Beacon, Boston, MA, 1974.
DERBY, LAVEY, 'Outreach, Intermarriage and Jewish Continuity', *Journal of Jewish Community Service*, Vol.68, No.4 (Summer 1992), pp.331–5.
DERSHOWITZ, ALAN, *Chutzpah*, Little, Brown, Boston, MA, 1991.
DON-YEHIYAH, ELIEZER, 'Galut in Zionist Ideology and in Israeli Society', in Eliezer Don-Yehiya (ed.), *Israel and Diaspora Jewry: Ideological and Political Perspectives*, Bar Ilan University Press, Jerusalem, 1991, pp.219–57.
EISEN, ARNOLD, *Galut: Modern Jewish Reflections on Homelessness and Homecoming*, Indiana University Press, Bloomington, IN, 1986.
—— 'An All-Volunteer Jewry', *Hadassah Magazine*, Vol.74, No.10 (1993), pp.18–21.

ELAZAR, DANIEL, *People and Polity*, Wayne State University Press, Detroit, MI, 1989.
—— 'The Role of Voluntary Leadership in Jewish Education', paper presented at the World Conference for Jewish Education, Jerusalem, 1984.
FEIN, LEONARD, *Where are We? The Inner Life of America's Jews*, Harper and Row, New York, 1988.
FINESTEIN, ISRAEL, *Jewish Society in Victorian England*, Vallentine Mitchell, London, 1993.
FISHMAN, SYLVIA BARACK and GOLDSTEIN, ALICE, 'When they are Grown Up They Will Not Depart: Jewish Education and the Jewish Behaviour of American Adults', *CMJS Research Report 8*, Brandeis University and the Jewish Education Service of North America, March 1993.
FRANKEL, JONATHAN and ZIPPERSTEIN, STEVEN J. (eds), *Assimilation and Community: The Jews in Nineteenth Century Europe*, Cambridge University Press, 1992.
GERSHENSON, ELLIOT, 'Will our Grandchildren be Jewish? No More Rhetoric', *Journal of Jewish Community Service*, Vol.68, No.4 (Summer 1992), pp.347–9.
GLAZER, NATHAN, *American Judaism*, University of Chicago Press, Chicago, IL, 1972.
GOLDBERG, J.J., 'America's Vanishing Jews', *Jerusalem Report*, 5 November 1992, pp.28–32.
GOLDSCHEIDER, CALVIN, *The American Jewish Community*, Brown University Press, 1986.
—— *Jewish Continuity and Change*, Indiana University Press, Bloomington, IN, 1986.
GOLDSCHEIDER, CALVIN and ZUCKERMAN, ALAN, *The Transformation of the Jews*, University of Chicago Press, Chicago, IL, 1984.
GORDIS, DAVID and BEN-HORIN, YOAV, *Jewish Identity in America*, University of Judaism, Los Angeles, 1991.
HALKIN, HILLEL, *Letters to an American Jewish Friend*, Jewish Publication Society, Philadelphia, PA, 1977.
HALPERN, BEN, *The American Jew: A Zionist Analysis*, Schocken, New York, 1983.
HERTZBERG, ARTHUR, 'The Emancipation: A Reassessment after Two Centuries', *Modern Judaism* Vol.1, No.2 (1982), pp.23–52.
—— (ed.), *The Zionist Idea*, Atheneum, New York, 1981.
HIMMELFARB, MILTON, *The Jews of Modernity*, Basic Books, New York, 1973.
JEWISH EDUCATIONAL DEVELOPMENT TRUST, *Securing our Future: Jewish Education in the United Kingdom*, London, 1992.
JEWISH OBSERVER, 'Continuity versus Eternity', *Jewish Observer*, March 1993, pp.19–22.
JOHNSON, PAUL, *A History of the Jews*, Weidenfeld & Nicolson, London, 1987.

KALMS, STANLEY, *A Time for Change: United Synagogue Review*, London, 1992.
KOSMIN, BARRY, 'Exploring and Understanding the Findings of the 1990 National Jewish Population Survey', paper prepared for Hollander Colloquium, July 1991.
KOSMIN, BARRY, and LEVY, KAREN, *Jewish Identity in an Anglo-Jewish Community*, Board of Deputies, London, 1983.
—— *Synagogue Membership in the United Kingdom 1983*, Board of Deputies, London, 1983.
KOSMIN, BARRY, et al., *Highlights of the CJF 1990 National Jewish Population Survey*, Council of Jewish Federations, New York, 1991.
KOSMIN, BARRY and WATERMAN, S., *British Jewry in the Eighties*, Board of Deputies, London, 1986.
LAUER, CHAIM, 'Planning, Advocacy and Funding for the Future of Jewish Education', *Jewish Spectator*, Winter 1992-93, pp.13–17.
LEADER, JEFFREY, 'Jewish Family Education: A British Initiative', unpublished report, London, 1992.
LENSKI, G., *The Religious Factor*, Doubleday, New York, 1961.
LEVITT, JOY, 'Will our Grandchildren be Jewish?', *Journal of Jewish Community Service*, Vol.68, No.4 (Summer 1992), pp.342–6.
LIEBMAN, CHARLES, *The Ambivalent American Jew*, Jewish Publication Society, Philadelphia, PA, 1973.
—— *Deceptive Images: Toward a Redefinition of American Jewry*, Transaction Books, New Brunswick, NJ, 1988.
LIEBMAN, CHARLES, and COHEN, STEVEN M., *Two Worlds of Judaism: The Israeli and American Experiences*, Yale University Press, New Haven, 1990.
LIPSET, SEYMOUR MARTIN (ed.), *American Pluralism and the Jewish Community*, Transaction, New Brunswick, 1990.
LIPSTADT, DEBORAH, 'Benefits of Belonging', *Hadassah Magazine*, Vol.74, No.10 (1993), pp.14–17.
MEDDING, PETER et al., 'Jewish Identity in Conversionary and Mixed Marriages', American Jewish Committee Jewish Sociology Papers, 1992.
MEYER, EGON, *Love and Tradition: Marriages between Jews and Christians* Schocken, New York, 1987.
NEUSNER, JACOB, *Stranger at Home*, University of Chicago Press, Chicago, IL, 1981.
—— *Israel in America*, Beacon, Boston, MA, 1985.
—— 'The Foundations of Jewish Existence', unpublished lecture, 1993.
REIMER, JOSEPH, *The Synagogue as a Context for Jewish Education*, Commission on Jewish Education in North America, 1990.
ROSENAK, MICHAEL (ed.), *Studies in Jewish Education*, Vol.2, Magnes Press, Jerusalem, 1984.

SACKS, JONATHAN, *Arguments for the Sake of Heaven*, Jason Aronson, Northvale, NJ, 1991.
—— 'Religious and National Identity: British Jewry and the State of Israel', in Eliezer Don-Yehiya (ed.), *Israel and Diaspora Jewry: Ideological and Political Perspectives*, Bar Ilan University Press, Jerusalem, 1991, pp.53–60.
—— *Crisis and Covenant: Jewish Thought after the Holocaust*, Manchester University Press, Manchester, 1992.
—— *One People? Tradition, Modernity and Jewish Unity*, Littman Library of Jewish Civilization, London, 1993.
—— 'A Decade of Jewish Renewal', Office of the Chief Rabbi, London, 1991.
—— 'A Time for Renewal: A Rabbinic Response to the Kalms Report', Office of the Chief Rabbi, London, 1991.
SCHIFF, ALVIN, *Jewish Supplementary Schooling: An Educational System in Need of Change*, Board of Jewish Education, New York, 1988.
SCHMOOL, MARLENA, 'Synagogue Marriages in Britain in the 1980s', *Jewish Journal of Sociology* Vol.33, No.2 (1991).
SCHMOOL, MARLENA, and COHEN, FRANCES, *British Synagogue Membership in 1990*, Board of Deputies, London, 1991.
SCHMOOL, MARLENA, and MILLER, STEVEN, 'Jewish Education and Identity Among London Synagogue Members', unpublished lecture, 1993.
SHINDLER, JULIAN, 'Marriage Trends in Anglo-Jewry: Where Do We Go From Here?', *Le'ela*, Vol.35 (1993), pp.19–22.
SHLUKER, DAVID, 'The Communal Education Restructuring Conundrum,' *Journal of Jewish Community Service*, Vol.68, No.3 (Spring 1992), pp.239–52.
SHRAGE, BARRY, 'A Communal Response to the Challenges of the 1990 CJF National Jewish Population Survey', *Journal of Jewish Community Service*, Vol.68, No.4 (Summer 1992), pp.321–30.
SILBERMAN, CHARLES, *A Certain People: American Jews and Their Lives Today*, Summit Books, New York, 1985.
WAXMAN, CHAIM I., *America's Jews in Transition*, Temple University Press, Philadelphia, 1983.
—— *American Aliyah: Portrait of an Innovative Migration Movement*, Wayne State University Press, Detroit, 1989.
WOOCHER, JONATHAN, *Sacred Survival: The Civil Religion of American Jews*, Indiana University Press, Bloomington, IN, 1986.
—— 'Jewish Education: Crisis and Vision', unpublished lecture, 1988.
—— 'Planning for Jewish Continuity', unpublished lecture, 1993.
—— 'Jewish Survival Tactics', *Hadassah Magazine*, Vol.74, No.10 (1993), pp.10–13.

Index

Abraham, 4, 13, 14, 15, 20, 34, 36, 37, 95, 112–13, 116
 and the next generation, 106–10
 why chosen, 35
Adler, Hermann, 65
Adler, Nathan Marcus, 65, 77, 79
Adorno, Theodor, 11
Akiva, Rabbi, 36
Aliyah, 18, 87, 92
 and religious commitment, 98
 new forms of, 97
Alkalai, Yehudah, 88
American Jewry, 14, 15, 17–19, 21–4, 34, 46, 50, 51, 57, 61, 66–9, 74, 91, 92, 95, 99, 107
Anglo-Jewry, 2, 3, 15, 18–20, 22, 23, 49, 55–8, 61, 68, 69, 71, 72, 90, 93, 94, 96, 103, 104, 107, 109–10, 119, 122, 123
 demographic losses, 2, 25
Anti-Zionism, 67, 87, 92, 119
antisemitism, 3, 27, 33, 34, 38, 50, 61, 65–8, 73, 74, 76–81, 88–93, 101, 117, 119
 and Jewish survival, 32–4
Aristotle, 107
Arnold, Matthew, 82
assimilation, 3, 5, 15, 31, 33, 34, 40, 42, 59, 66, 75, 76, 89, 94, 96
Association of Jewish Sixth Formers, 56
Auschwitz, 45, 46, 80

bagel, the assimilating, 22
Bar Kochba rebellion, 15, 39, 43
Barth, Karl, 10
Bayme, Dr Steven, 74
Bellah, Robert, 80
Ben Gurion, 45
Benjamin of Tudela, 53
Berdyayev, Nicolas, 9
Berlin, Irving, 95
Berlin, Isaiah, 11
bet midrash, 53
birthrate, Jewish, 20

Board of Deputies, 18, 68, 90
Borochov, Ber, 96
Brodetsky, Selig, 90

Canetti, Elias, 11
census, 28
Chagall, 11
Chajes, Zvi Hirsch, 19
charity
 aims of, 51
Chmielnicki massacres, 33, 54
Chomsky, Noam, 11
citizenship, duties of, 52
cognitive dissonance, 108
Cohen, Steven, 66, 97
conversion
 to Christianity, 14
 to Judaism, 24
Council of Jewish Federations, 17
crusades, 12, 33
Cuddihy, John Murray, 64
Cyrus, 41

Damascus Blood Libel, 88, 114
David, King, 28, 29, 47
 as a symbol of the Jewish people, 39–40
Dayan, Eli, 59
Dead Sea Scrolls, 44
demography
 Torah's perspective on, 28
Dershowitz, Alan, 4
Descartes, 35
Deuteronomy, 37
diaspora, 1–3, 14, 15, 18–20, 23, 25, 28, 30, 38, 42, 45–8, 58, 59, 61, 66, 68, 69, 73, 86–100, 102, 104, 106, 110, 116, 119, 121, 122
 and Israel, 86–100
 Jewish identity in, 38, 98
 negation of, *see Shelilat ha-golah*
 survival of, 86–7
Disraeli, Benjamin, 65
divine providence, 32
divorce
 rates of Jewish, 23

Dreyfus affair, 87, 89
Dubnow, Simon, 96

education, 35, 39, 41–4, 45–8, 52–8, 65, 71–2, 98, 101, 103, 104, 106–7, 108–10, 118, 120–3
  see also Jewish education
Einstein, Albert, 11
Eisen, Arnold, 91
Elazar, Daniel, 19, 40
Eliot, George, 78
Esau, 20
Essenes, 44, 46
Esther, book of, 26
Ethiopian Jewry, 50, 68, 71
Exodus, 2, 28, 37, 70
Ezekiel, 34, 63
Ezra, 20, 41–2, 45, 76
  the teacher as hero, 43

Fackenheim, Emil, 14
Fein, Leonard, 66
Finestein, Israel, 65
Fishman, Sylvia Barack, 47
four sons
  in the *Haggadah*, 60
fourth generation, 21, 59–62, 103
'fourth-generation phenomenon', 60
freewill, 33
Freud, Sigmund, 11
Frost, Robert, 92

Genesis, 2, 28, 37
Ger, *Rebbe* of, 60
Goethe, Johann von, 78
Golden Calf, 49, 105
Goldscheider, Calvin, 69
Goldstein, Alice, 47
Gordon, A.D., 96
Graetz, Heinrich, 32

Hagar, 112
Haman, 16, 26, 114
Hanukkah, 40
Harman, David, 99
Hebrew language
  of prayer, 11
  rebirth of, 15
  and Israel, 98
Heilman, Samuel, 75, 81, 84
Heine, Heinrich, 14, 24, 33, 81
Hellenisation, 40, 76
Henoch of Alexander, Rabbi, 18

Herzl, Theodor, 73, 89, 90, 92
Herzog, Chaim, 59
Herzog, Elizabeth, 36
Herzog, Yaakov, 76
Hess, Moses, 88, 89
Hildesheimer, Azriel, 77
Hillel, 36, 51
Himmelfarb, Milton, 13, 29
Hirsch, Samson Raphael, 77, 78, 79
Hitler, 14, 45, 68, 114
Holocaust, 3, 7, 10, 14, 16, 25, 27, 44–7, 50, 51, 66, 67, 69, 70, 72, 74, 79–82, 87, 90, 93, 97, 101, 105, 111
  responses to, 45
  and the imperative of Jewish survival, 15, 25

identity
  as reality internalised, 36
  integration, 3, 64, 66
  and the challenge of emancipation, 64
  and the crisis of identity, 64
  from integration to survival, 66
  in Britain, 65
intermarriage, 2, 17, 20, 75
  in America, 21
  in Anglo-Jewry, 18, 22
  in Denver, 21
  in Los Angeles, 21
  in Phoenix, 21
  stigma attached to, 21
  the only effective argument against, 102–3
Isaac, 20, 113
Isaiah, 8, 36, 98
Ishmael, 112
Israel and the diaspora, 86–100
  from conflict to convergence, 95–8
Israel, people of
  see Jewish people
Israel, State of, 3, 7, 29, 44, 50, 59, 67–9, 73–4, 90–2
  and continuity, 86–7, 98–100
  and Jewish survival, 87–8
  and the renewal of diaspora life, 91, 99
  Israeli attitudes towards diaspora, 96

Jacob
  and Jewish identity, 3
Jakobovits, Lord, 57
Jeremiah, 8, 32, 38, 52, 63, 77
Jerusalem, 15, 36, 38, 39, 41, 99
Jerusalem Report, 17

Index

Jewish continuity, 3–5, 14, 15, 19, 21, 23, 25, 27, 30, 34, 39, 40, 41, 47, 49, 50, 59–61, 72, 73–4, 86, 87, 98, 101–11, 116, 117–23
and education, 31–48, 106–7
crisis of, 3, 14, 23, 59, 64
different from integration and survival, 73
era of, 71, 73
in the diaspora, 87
lack of strategy for, 50
mystery of, 114
secret of, 39
Jewish Continuity, 4, 101–11, 117–23
mission statement, 106–7
objectives of, 119–23
organisational style, 109
Jewish creativity, 11, 12
Jewish Darwinism, 104
Jewish education
and doing, 106
and continuity, 107
and reinforcement, 108
coverage, 108
first century BCE, 52
first century CE, 52
in the days of Ezra, 42
in Victorian England, 65
in the second century BCE, 42
in the age of integration, 71
in medieval Europe, 53
in fifteenth-century Spain, 53
in the *shtetl*, 36
Judaism's culture of study, 36
lack of strategy, 104, 108
priority over other causes, 52
research on impact of, 47
Jewish Educational Development Trust, 55, 57
Jewish expulsions, 11
Jewish identity, 75
and a sense of history, 62
and future-orientation, 37
and inner-directedness, 37
and love of freedom, 116
and patrilineal descent, 69
and renewal of memory, 37
and surrounding cultures, 36
and survivalism, 72
and the love of children, 116
as a religious vocation, 37
as an ethnic group, 68
confusion of, 23

in Israel, 38
in the diaspora, 38, 39, 122
Israel and diaspora compared, 23, 99
living between two worlds, 95
now needs to be created, 106
persistence of for three generations, 61
religious or national?, 90
transmission of, 14
Jewish people, 1–3, 7–18, 20, 22–50, 52, 53, 57–60, 63–85, 101–11, 115, 116, 121–3
a nation of educators, 35
distinctiveness maintained, 13
losing its will to survive, 2
united in crisis, 2
Jewish population
history of, 29
Jews' Free School, 71
Johanan ben Zakkai, 43–5
Johnson, Paul, 2, 9, 12, 27, 36
Josephus, 43, 52
Joshua ben Gamla, Rabbi, 52
Joshua, Rabbi, 34
Jubilee, 63
Judaism, 1, 2, 4, 10, 12, 23–6, 33–5, 37, 43–6, 51, 52, 60, 63, 64, 73, 84, 97, 98, 99, 103, 115, 119
a collective faith, 3
a religion of continuity, 34
and counting time, 63
and Greek civilisation, 13
and the sanctity of life, 115
ethical message of, 12, 13

Kafka, Franz, 11
Kagan, Israel Meir, 80
Kalischer, Rabbi Zvi Hirsch, 88
Kamenetzky, Jacob, 45
Katznelson, Berl, 96
Klatzkin, Jacob, 89
Koestler, Arthur, 81, 92
Kook, Rabbi Abraham, 89, 105
Kook, Rabbi Zvi Yehuda, 90
Kosmin, Barry, 18, 20, 23
Kotler, Rabbi Aaron, 45

Lazarus, Emma, 95
Lenski, Gerhard, 67
Lévi-Strauss, Claude, 11
Luther, Martin, 27

Maccabees, 40
Mahler, Gustav, 11, 81

Maimonides, Rabbi Moses, 11, 36, 51, 52
Marseilles, 53
Marx, Karl, 11
Mendlowitz, Rabbi Shragai, 45
Merneptah, 6, 114
Mesha, 6, 114
Messiah, 43
Mishneh Torah, 52
Modigliani, Amedeo, 11
monotheism, 12
Montefiore, Sir Moses, 65, 79
Moses, 7, 8, 20, 28, 34–6, 63, 99, 105

Nachman, Rabbi, 81
Napoleon, 38
National Jewish Population Survey (1990), 17, 18, 21, 23, 47
Nehemiah, 20, 41, 76
Neusner, Jacob, 119
Nietzsche, Friedrich, 10, 27, 78
Nordau, Max, 33, 89
North American Jewish Data Bank, 18

Omer, counting of, 63
One People?, 1, 105
Operation Exodus, 74
Operation Moses, 74

Pascal, Blaise, 9, 27
Peres, Shimon, 1
Pharaoh, 114
Pharisees, 44, 46
philanthropy, Jewish, 50
  in Anglo-Jewry, 55
  low priority to education, 56
  priority of domestic causes, 51
Pinsker, Yehuda Leib, 89
Pissarro, Camille, 11
Pittsburgh Platform of 1885, 66
Plato, 107
Posquières, 53
prophecy
  and prediction, 32
  and the sense of history, 63
Proust, Marcel, 11

Qumran sect, 44

Rabbi
  as teacher, 35
Rachel, 34
Rashi, 11, 36
Rava, 35, 53

Rebekah, 20
Redbridge Report, 18, 20
Reform Judaism, in America, 24
Reines, Rabbi Isaac, 96
Resh Lakish, 33–4
responsibility, personal and collective, 52
Rotenstreich, Natan, 90
Reisman, David, 37

Sadducees, 44, 46
Sanctuary, 49
Sandberg, Neil, 21
Sarah, 4, 14, 112–13
Schiff, Alvin, 123
Schneersohn, Rabbi Menachem Mendel, 45, 105
Schoenberg, Arnold, 11
Scholem, Gershom, 90
Schweid, Eliezer, 90
Securing Our Future (1992), 57
Shelilat ha-golah (negation of the diaspora), 88–91
Shimon ben Shetach, 52
Shindler, Julian, 23
Shokeid, Moshe, 96
Silberman, Charles, 24, 69
Six Day War, 50, 66, 90
Soloveitchik, Rabbi Joseph, 45, 78, 105
Soutine, Chaim, 11
Soviet Union, 8
Spanish expulsion, 26, 29
Spinoza, Benedict, 11, 32, 33
Steinsaltz, Adin, 80
Sunday Times, 18
survival, Jewish, 2, 3, 7, 10, 11, 20, 26, 31, 33, 35, 41, 43, 45, 51, 66–8, 72–4, 87–8, 94, 96, 105, 116
  collective or selective, 105
  effects of survivalism, 68
  shortcomings of as identity, 69
  story of Jewish, 7–16
  the new survivalism, 66
synagogue marriages
  fall in number of, 18
Syrkin, Nahman, 96

Tam, Rabbenu, 53
Temple
  destruction of the first, 41
  destruction of the second, 42
Titus, 42
Tolstoy, Leo, 78

Torah
 and eternal life, 9
 the portable homeland of the Jew, 36
Toynbee, Arnold, 10
transformationist sociology, Jewish, 69
Twain, Mark, 31, 34
Twersky, Isidore, 73
Tzedaka, 51

United Jewish Appeal, 17
United Synagogue, 56, 57, 68
university chaplaincy, 48, 118

Valladolid synod, 53
Vespasian, 42, 43
Vital, David, 97

Warsaw Ghetto uprising, 39, 66
Weizman, Ezer, 86, 88
Wells, H.G., 52
'Who is a Jew?', 1
Wittgenstein, Ludwig, 11
Woocher, Jonathan, 117, 120

Yavneh, 43
Yehoshua, A.B., 98
Yerida (emigration from Israel), 92, 96
Yerushalmi, Yosef Hayim, 63
Yeshiva, 53

Zborowski, Mark, 36
Zionism, 73, 87, 88–90, 96, 97
Zionist Congress, first, 90
Zionist Federation Educational Trust, 56